Philipp Grollmann, Dietmar Frommberger, Ute Clement,
Thomas Deißinger, Uwe Lauterbach, Matthias Pilz, Georg Spöttl (Eds.)

International Handbook of Vocational Education and Training

Antje Wessels | Matthias Pilz

India

Issue 50
Volume 24

Citation:

Wessels, Antje; Pilz, Matthias: India. International Handbook of Vocational Education and Training. Editors: Grollmann, Philipp; Frommberger, Dietmar; Clement, Ute; Deißinger, Thomas; Lauterbach, Uwe; Pilz, Matthias; Spöttl, Georg. Bonn 2018

1st edition 2018

Publisher:

Federal Institute for Vocational Education and Training
Robert-Schuman-Platz 3
D-53175 Bonn
Web: www.bibb.de

Publication management:

Strategic office "Publications and Scientific Information Services"
Email: publikationsmanagement@bibb.de
www.bibb.de/veroeffentlichungen

Production:

Verlag Barbara Budrich
Stauffenbergstraße 7
D-51379 Leverkusen
Web: www.budrich.de
Email: info@budrich.de

eISBN 978-3-96208-077-8
ISBN 978-3-8474-2247-1

Bibliographic information from the German National Library

The German National Library catalogues this publication in the German National Bibliography. Detailed information is available online at http://dnb.ddb.de.

Editorial

India is a country with an emerging economy. It extends from the Himalayas to the Indian Ocean and is the word's seventh biggest nation. The Republic of India is home to 1.3 billion people in 29 states. The ethnic diversity is vast, and brings with it a huge number of different languages and religious affiliations. You are just as likely to come across extremes of social inequality and poverty as you are wealth and a growing middle class.

Compulsory schooling does exist for children aged 6 to 14, however the actual school attendance rate is extremely mixed, particularly in rural regions. Due to the responsibility of the states for education, huge disparities are present in the education system. At the same time, economic growth is strong. Over recent years, growth of the gross national product has been well over five per cent. Key industrial sectors include the textile industry, iron and steel production and the chemicals industry. Information technology and the service sector are growing. The highest rates of employment are to be found in agriculture, while at the same time its share of the gross national product is relatively low. Commercial life is shaped by the informal sector.

The issue of training skilled workers is the highest priority for India, and this is also due to the rapidly increasing population. On the one hand, there is a high demand for trained skilled workers. On the other hand, training for the labour market is key to the integration of young adults. However, vocational education and training also has a lower status in India compared to general education and university level education and training. Intensive efforts are being made to reform vocational education and training, and, gradually, successes are becoming apparent.

Using this country study to present vocational education and training in India and explain it to readers is particularly important for international comparative research in vocational education and training. For India, no similar product is available in this detailed and systematic form. It is a pleasure to read this country study and gain an impression of the VET situation in India.

This study is published in English and accompanies the German edition of the study in the German language publication "Internationales Handbuch der Berufsbildung" (International Handbook of Vocational Education and Training).

Provided that the capacities are available, the editing team for the International Handbook of Vocational Education and Training will aim to make country studies, which also internationally have something unique to offer, available to the much broader English-language readership.

Bonn, Osnabrück, Bremen, Frankfurt am Main, Kassel, Cologne and Constance

On behalf of the editors
Philipp Grollmann and Dietmar Frommberger

Contents

Indices of tables and figures

Index of tables

Index of figures

Basic data [2017]

Republic of India/भारत गणराज्य (Bhārat Gaṇarājya)/IN

Area [km²]	2,973,190 [2015]	
Population density [inhabitants/km²]	441 [2015]	
Inhabitants [1,000]	1,311,051 [2015]	
Age [proportion of total population] [in %]	100.0	
0–14 years	28.2 [2015]	
15–64 years	65.6 [2015]	
65 and older	5.6 [2015]	
Working age population [population aged 15 and older] [in %]	53.7 [2015]	
Labour supply [1,000]	501,612 [2015]	
Total [in % of the age group] total	m	f
Aged 15 and above	76.4 [2015]	25.8 [2015]
Unemployment rate [in %]	3.5 [2015]	
Youth unemployment rate [in %]	9.7 [2015]	

Main economic focuses [2015] [in %]

Sector	Labour demand [in %]	Gross added value [in % of GDP]
Primary/agriculture and forestry, fishery	49.7 [2013]	17.0 [2015]
Secondary/manufacturing industry	21.5 [2013]	29.7 [2015]
Tertiary/services	28.7 [2013]	53.2 [2015]

Economic performance [2015] [in US$]

Gross Domestic Product (GDP)	2,073,002 million
Gross Domestic Product per capita	1,604

(Destatis 2017)

Abbreviations

Abbreviation	Meaning (Explanation)
AA	Accredited Agencies
AHI	Apex Hi-Tech Institute (Training programme for trainers)
AICTE	All India Council for Technical Education
AITT	All India Trade Test
AM	Advanced Modules
ASSOCHAM	Associated Chambers of Commerce and Industry of India
ATI	Advanced Training Institute
ATS	Apprenticeship Training Scheme
AVTS	Advanced Vocational Training Scheme
BBBT	Broad Based Basic Training
BIBB	Bundesinstitut für Berufsbildung – Federal Institute for Vocational Education and Training
BMBF	Bundesministerium für Bildung und Forschung – Federal Ministry of Education and Research
BMZ	Bundesministerium für wirtschaftliche Zusammenarbeit und Entwicklung – Federal Ministry for Economic Cooperation and Development
BoPT	Board of Practical Training
BTC	Basic Training Centre
BVTC	Bosch Vocational Training Centre
B.Ed.	Bachelor of Education
B.T.	Bachelor of Teaching
B.Voc.	Bachelor of Vocation
CABE	Central Board of Education
CAC	Central Apprentice Council
CBSE	Central Board of Secondary Education
CEC	Continuing Education Centre
CII	Confederation of Indian Industry
CIMI	Central Instructional Media Institute
CISCE	Council for the Indian School Certificate Examinations

CITS	Craft Instructor Training Scheme
CoE	Centre of Excellence
COPA	Computer Operator and Programming Assistant
CSR	Corporate Social Responsibility
CSTARI	Central Staff Training & Research Institute
CTI	Craftsmen Training Institute
CTS	Craftsmen Training Scheme
DGT	Directorate of Training
DVET	Directorate of Vocational Education and Training
FICCI	Federation of Indian Chambers of Commerce and Industry
FTI	Foreman Training Institute (Master craftsman school)
GCSE	General Certificate of Secondary Education
GTTI	Gedee Technical Training Institute
HSSC	Higher Secondary School Certificate
IAT	Institut für Arbeitswissenschaft und Technologiemanagement – Institute for Work Science and Technology Management
ICT	Information and communication technologies
IGCC	Indo-German Chamber of Commerce
IIM	Indian Institute of Management
IISERs	Indian Institute of Science Education and Research
IIT	Indian Institute of Technology
ILP	Initial learning programme
IMC	Institutional Management Committee
IT	Information technology
ITC	Industrial Training Centre
ITES	Information Technology Enabled Services
ITI	Industrial Training Institute
IToTS	Institutes for Training of Teachers
JSS	Jan Shikshan Sansthan (Institute of People's Education)
KVIC	Khadi and Village Industries Commission (Training institution for small and medium-sized companies focusing on Khadi (handwoven clothing) and village industries)
KVK	Krishi Vigyan Kendras (Agricultural Extension Centre) (Agricultural advisory service)

MES	Modular Employable Skills
MHRD	Ministry of Human Resources Development
MoLE	Ministry of Labour and Employment
MoRD	Ministry of Rural Development
MSDE	Ministry of Development and Entrepreneurship
NAC	National Apprenticeship Certificate
NAPS	National Apprenticeship Promotion Scheme
NCERT	National Council of Educational Research and Training
NCVT	National Council of Vocational Training
NGO	Non-Governmental Organisation
NIOS	National Institute for Open Schooling
NIT	National Institute of Technology
NLM	National Literacy Mission
NOS	National Occupational Standards
NPE	National Policy on Education
NPSD	National Policy on Skill Development
NRLM	Aajeevika National Rural Livelihood Mission (Project to combat poverty)
NSDA	National Skill Development Agency
NSDC	National Skill Development Corporation
NSDF	National Skill Development Fund
NSDM	National Skill Development Mission
NSP	National Skill Policy
NSQF	National Skills Qualifications Framework
NSSO	National Sample Survey Organisation
NTC	National Trade Certificate
NVEQF	National Vocational Education Qualifications Framework
NVQF	National Vocational Qualifications Framework
NVTI	National Vocational Training Institute
OBC	Other Backward Castes
OBE	Open Basic Education Programmes
OECD	Organisation for Economic Cooperation and Development
PCP	Personal Contact Programmes

PMKVY	Pradhan Mantri Kaushal Vikas Yojana (Programme within the scope of the Skill Development Initiative)
PoT	Principle of Teaching
PPP	Public-private partnership
PSSCIVE	Pandit Sunderlal Sharma Central Institute of Vocational Education (Training provider for research, development and training in vocational education)
PwD	Persons with disabilities
QP	Qualification Packages
RIC	Related Instruction Centre
RMSA	Rashriya Madhyamik Shiksa Abhiyan (Funding programme within the scope of the Skill Development Initiative)
RPL	Recognition of Prior Learning
RTE	Right to Education
RUSA	Rashtriya Uchchattar Shiksha Abhiyan (Funding programme within the scope of the Skill Development Initiative)
RVA	Recognition, Validation and Accreditation Process
RVTI	Regional Vocational Training Institute
SC	Scheduled Castes
SCERT	State Council of Education Research and Training
SCVE	State Councils for Vocational Education
SCVT	State Councils of Vocational Training
SDI	Skills Development Initiatives Scheme
SGSY	Swarnajayanti Gram Swarozgar Yojna (Education and training programme)
SM	Specialised Module
SSA	Sarva Shiksha Abhiyan (Universalisation of elementary education)
SSC	Sector Skill Councils (Autonomous committees headed by industry to manage skills development, comparable to the German chambers)
ST	Scheduled Tribes (Registered underprivileged tribes)

TCS	TATA Consultancy Service (TATA is an Indian automobile manufacturer)
TM	Training Methodology
TT	Trade Technology
TVET	Technical Vocational Education and Training
UG	Undergraduate
UGC	University Grants Commission
UNDP	United Nations Development Programme
UNESCO	United Nations Educational, Scientific and Cultural Organisation
UNEVOC	International Centre for Technical and Vocational Education and Training (UNESCO)
VET	Vocational education and training
VTIP	Vocational Training Improvement Projects
VTP	Vocational training provider
WITIs	Women Industrial Training Institutes

Introduction and summary

For many European visitors, India is an exotic land which is difficult to understand in a multitude of regards. The way in which the country is perceived is characterised by a certain sense of ambivalence. On the one hand, India's magical colours and smells, graceful people, deep sense of religiousness and spirituality, and wonderful landscapes are all extolled. On the other hand, there is a bemoaning of the negative excesses of mega cities such as Mumbai (Bombay), Kolkata (Calcutta) and Chennai (Madras) and of the increasing environmental pollution. Extreme poverty, child labour and the disadvantages that women still suffer in parts of public life and in the family are further objects of criticism (see Imhasly 2015). In literary terms, these ambivalences have been particularly impressively portrayed in the highly readable novel "A Fine Balance" by Rohinton Mistry.

India is a country of contradictions, a fact which is memorably enshrined in the "Incredible India" slogan propagated by the Indian Tourist Board. This is a land which takes on enormous dimensions in terms of both geographical extent and population size. The consequence is that a host of different ethnicities, cultures, languages and religions all form an integral part of everyday Indian life. Social hierarchies, defined by the caste system in particular, still play a major role today (see Imhasly 2015).

From the foreign point of view, account needs to be taken of the fact that India has undergone considerable change in both economic and political terms since the 1990s. It is only from this time onwards that comprehensive reforms and the economic development of the country have noticeably gained momentum at many levels (see below). As a result, the outcomes of political reforms and initiatives are only just slowly becoming visible, and many effects require further time for implementation. Consequently, foreign observers need to exercise the very highest degree of caution in evaluating and assessing these developments.

Vocational education and training in India has been a focus for German stakeholders since the 1990s at least. Firstly, various German companies have established production facilities in India or else are witnessing the emergence of significant sales markets in the country. The securing of a supply of qualified young skilled workers at a local level is of crucial significance to these firms. Secondly, state agencies, relevant project providers and academic research institutions have all acted as vehicles in bringing about an increase in the area of VET cooperation.

The field of vocational education and training also illustrates the dimensions which aspects such as policy initiatives are beginning to assume in India. A Skills Initiative instigated by the Central Government (see Chapter 5.8.2) has, for example, been launched with the intention of providing training or continuing training for 500 million people by the year 2022 (see NSDC year of publication not stated.)

Against this background, the aim of the present country study is to help provide a compact insight into all those interested in VET issues in India.

At this point, we would like to indicate a small number of aspects that are of vital importance to the presentation and analysis.

The first point that needs to be mentioned is that the concept of the "occupation" as used in German-speaking countries does not exist in India. Nevertheless, the term "occupation" will still be used in order to offer readers appropriate points of reference. The text below also provides extensive explanations in order to enable the respective VET activities to be correctly interpreted from a German point of view.

Attention also needs to be drawn to the fact that vocational education and training in India is organised in a highly differentiated and indeed sometimes diffuse way. A multitude of various programmes exists both at national and federal state level. Some of these are implemented for a few years only and are reformed at very frequent intervals. India's strong preference for using acronyms to designate programmes can make things even more difficult to understand. This country study attempts to portray major vocational education and training initiatives in a way that is as structurally clear as possible. The acronyms used are listed in the index of abbreviations.

Clear presentation is further exacerbated by the fact that India has a multitude of political stakeholders who operate at federal and/or individual state level. Initial distribution of areas of responsibility between the national state level and across the individual federal states extends into a jumble of competencies and disputed VET remits between various ministries and their downstream institutions, again both federally and at state level.

In terms of content, consideration must be accorded to at least four specific characteristics within the Indian context which exert a strong influence on the structuring of VET and are an object of detailed discussion in the remarks set out below.

The first thing that needs to be taken into account is that India was a British Colony until 1947. The country's colonial rulers left a significant mark on many areas of economic and societal life and on the educational system.[1] Although Indians now point with pride to the developments they have achieved themselves, some important basic structures dating back to colonial times are still in existence. These include the design of the secondary school system, which continues to have an impact on vocational education and training up to the present day.

The second characteristic is closely allied to and reinforces the first. In an entirely similar way to developments in the British system, the trend towards academisation in India continues unabated. The high degree of esteem enjoyed by academic education as

---

1   This has produced one benefit with regard to the research carried out for this country study. In contrast to many other countries, English is commonly used as an official language in India and is also dominant within the context of research. This makes it easier to understand the relevant sources of information, and the bibliography appended includes both German-language secondary sources and original English-language sources from India.

opposed to the low status assigned to vocational education and training programmes is also determined by India's cultural and religious history rather than merely by the British occupation. Tradition allocates physical work and all activities connected with any kind of uncleanliness to the lower castes. By the same token, office tasks are considered the measure of all things. For vocational education and training, the consequence is that training in technical and commercial private sector occupations is stigmatised and that commercial and administrative vocational education and training programmes offer only a limited appeal because such activities are predominantly performed by pre-academic or university graduates.

The third notable Indian characteristic also exhibits similarities to the Anglo-Saxon countries. This relates to the low level of interest shown by Indian companies in committing to VET or training measures for their employees in the intermediate skill sector (see Pilz 2016 b). Alongside the traditional view that vocational education and training primarily constitutes an individual or state task, this circumstance is also driven by the fact that the Indian labour market is extremely flexible and unregulated. In many cases, this produces high rates of staff turnover and engenders in employers a fear that they will suffer migration of employees and therefore also a loss of investment if relevant training is provided beforehand.

The last of the special characteristics outlined here refers to a circumstance specifically found in India. When describing the formal vocational education and training system, account needs to be taken of the fact that less than ten per cent of the Indian population are employed in the formal sector of the labour market at all. The part of the labour market which is denoted as the informal sector is dominant, the consequence being that most employees acquire their skills and knowledge in an area of the economy that is unregulated and therefore also unclear (see Jung/Pilz 2016). Such a background creates a further significant increase in complexity in terms of presenting the facts and circumstances that apply in India (see Chapter 4.6 for details).

Over the course of the past few years, the Indian government has recognised that the challenges within the area of vocational education and training are immense and urgently require a solution. The most striking example of this new perception of VET by the political establishment is the founding of the Ministry of Skill Development and Entrepreneurship (MSDE), which was instigated in 2014 by Prime Minister Narendra Modi and is now up and running (see MSDE 2015). The central objective of the MSDE is to focus the fragmented responsibilities in vocational education and training and thus launch more effective initiatives.

This country study takes account of the status that applied in 2016 and offers its readers an initial point of access to the complexity of vocational education and training in India. Further analysis of India's school, VET and employment system is provided in an edited volume authored by just under 20 experts on the country's education and entitled "India: Preparation for the World of Work – Education System and School to Work Transition" (Pilz 2016a).

1 Introduction to general geographical, societal, political and economic conditions

1.1 General social and cultural conditions

India has more than 1.3 billion inhabitants, the highest population of any country on earth after China. Annual population growth is stated to be 1.2 per cent (see GTAI 2016).

Table 1: Total population of India up to 2015

Year	Total population
1990	870,601,776
2000	1,053,481,072
2010	1,230,984,504
2011	1,247,446,011
2012	1,263,589,639
2013	1,279,498,874
2014	1,295,291,543
2015	1,311,050,527

Source: World Bank 2017a

India has an extremely young population. According to estimates, the average age of a worker in India in 2020 will be 29. By way of comparison, the corresponding average age in China is 37. In other industrialised countries, the average worker is aged over 45 (see Pilz 2016a, p. 8). Sixty-two per cent of the population are currently of working age. More than 54 per cent of the population as a whole are aged under 25 (see GoI 2015). This means that India is benefiting from the so-called demographic dividend, which is produced by an increasing proportion of persons of working age (aged between 15 and 59). The prognosis is that this is associated with an opportunity for continuous economic growth.

Table 2: Age structure in India up to 2015 [in %]

	0–14	15–64	65+
2004	33.19	62.09	4.72
2005	32.78	62.44	4.78
2006	32.43	62.72	4.85
2007	32.06	63.01	4.92
2008	31.69	63.32	4.99
2009	31.30	63.65	5.05
2010	30.89	63.99	5.11
2011	30.50	64.30	5.20
2012	30.08	64.63	5.29
2013	29.65	64.97	5.38
2014	29.21	65.30	5.49
2015	28.79	65.60	5.62

Source: World Bank, year of publication not stated

India's diversity of languages and religions and the country's caste system exert a particular influence on societal structure. Just less than three quarters of the population speak one of the widespread Indo-Aryan languages which are predominantly to be found in the North of India. Hindi is an Indo-Aryan language that is spoken by around one third of the population and is the only national official language besides English. Twenty-one regional languages are officially recognised, including Tamil, Marathi, Punjabi and Bengali (see Wessels 2012). Regional languages are of considerable significance both in everyday working life and in the primary and secondary educational sectors. In the wake of globalisation, English is gaining a high degree of importance in trade and industry and in the service sector as well as in tertiary education (see ibid.).

Table 3: Ethnic groups in India in 2000 [in %]

Indo-Aryan	Dravidian	Mongolian and other
72.0	25.0	3.0

Source: CIA, year of publication not stated

The degree of religious diversity and extensive peaceful coexistence is remarkable. No other country has as many different religions, deities and temples all enjoying equal recognition. More than 80 per cent of Indians are Hindus. About 13 per cent are Muslims, approximately 2.2 per cent are Christians and 1.9 per cent are Sikhs. The remaining population is made up of Buddhists, Jains, Parsis and others. The Hindu caste system extends back centuries and sub-divides Indian society into various groups, which previously performed the same occupation. Society is subject to a strict form of hierarchy up to the present day (see Wessels 2012; Debroy/Tellis/Reece 2014). The systematic order relates to four castes ("varnas", or "colours"). These are priests (brahman), warriors (kshatriya), traders and farmers (vaishya) and workers (shudra, today referred to as "backward caste"). The term used in India to denote a caste is, however, "jati". Jati denotes the community into which a person is born (see Rothermund 2008; Betz 1997). Beside the four castes that are accorded a fixed place within the hierarchy of Indian society and are identified by name and occupation, social identity in India is also characterised by a large number of sub-castes (see Wessels 2012; Vermeer/Neumann 2015). There are far in excess of 3,000 sub-castes and secondary castes, such as "other backward castes" and "untouchables" (dalits). This means that there are many "scheduled tribes". These sub-castes contain 15 per cent dalits and 8.2 per cent scheduled tribe members, meaning that they account for a significant proportion of Indian society (see Debroy/Tellis/Reece 2014). Although the caste system was officially abolished by the 1949 Constitution, it continues to have a societal influence and holds a high degree of importance in the political system. This will be looked at in more detail in the following chapter.

Further cultural and social characteristics which need to be further highlighted are poverty, rural flight, the role of women, child labour and illiteracy.

India is frequently associated with poverty. Despite continuous economic growth and the societal advancement this has brought, the 2013 United Nations Human Development Report states that 28.8 per cent of the population live in extreme poverty, whilst a further 16.4 per cent are at risk of poverty (see Kooperation International 2014). Malnutrition and an inadequate health service are only two indicators of poverty, and lack of education is not the least of the reasons why people live in impoverished circumstances (see Debroy/Tellis/Reece 2014).

India is also known for its mega cities such as Delhi, which has approximately 25 million inhabitants (see Bhatnagar 2014). Despite the rising population in agglomerations, about 70 per cent of poor population groups live in the countryside (see Debroy/Tellis/Reece 2014). According to information supplied by the government, the poorest 60 per cent of the rural population possess only five per cent of arable land. Such land is instead under the control of major owners and company groups (see bpb 2014a). An associated rural flight to India's metropolises can be observed. Many migrants from poverty hope to secure a better life and end up in the slums on the outskirts of the mega cities. The lack of prospects for many of those fleeing poverty means that involvement of children in working life is essential. Child labour and subsequent illiteracy are an established part of public life and make it more difficult to improve the situation of those affected (see bpb 2014a; Debroy/Tellis/Reece 2014).

Women in India continue to constitute a significantly disadvantaged group. In their everyday lives, women are forced to face discrimination and a lower social status (see

Debroy/Tellis/Reece 2014). The prevailing shortage of women (see Table 4) has been brought about by instances of human intervention. These range from the intentional abortion of female foetuses to neglect of young daughters-in-law (see Debroy/Tellis/ Reece 2014; Lang-Wojtasik 2013, p. 215). Discrimination against women is reflected in a lower school enrolment rate for girls than for boys (significantly higher proportion of illiteracy amongst women, see Table 5), a higher drop-out rate during school education because of family commitments (supporting the family, marriage whilst still young) and poorer payment in working life (see Debroy/Tellis/Reece 2014). Because of the ongoing and persistent unequal status of women, many programmes have been instigated by the government or by non-governmental organisations (NGOs) in an attempt to bring about improvement in their situation.

Table 4: Overall population in India by gender [in %]

	Women	Men
2000	48.20	51.80
2010	48.14	51.86
2015	48.17	51.83

Source: World Bank 2017b

Table 5: Literacy in India up to 2015 [in %]

	Women	Men	Total
1981	25.68	54.84	40.76
1991	33.73	61.64	48.22
2001	47.84	73.41	61.02
2006	50.82	75.19	62.75
2011	59.28	78.88	69.3
2015*	62.98	80.94	-

* The source does not provide any information on the overall rate of literacy for 2015.
Source: World Bank, year of publication not stated

Alongside these somewhat negative characteristics, India is also known for its films, music and literature. Cinema plays a particularly significant role in modern Indian socie-ty. The "Bollywood" brand is a world leader in terms of its number of film productions. Between 1,000 and 1,200 films are produced every year, twice as many as in Hollywood (see bpb 2014a).

1.2 General political and legal conditions

Historical development in India can be divided into various cultural epochs. These begin with the very earliest settlement (200,000 BC) and go on to encompass the Hindu Kingdoms (Magadha) of the 3rd century BC, the rule of the Muslim Mughal emperors (10th century), British colonial rule and the route to independence (see Betz 1997, p. 4). When independence took effect on 15 August 1947, the colony of India was divided and the country of Pakistan came into being. Over the course of time, the various cultural characteristics of India led to the firm delineation of federal states (see Vermeer/Neumann 2015, pp. 24 ff.), and these continue to form an established part of the country up to the present day. Because of diversity stretching back for many years (religion, language) and despite instances of resistance amongst some sections of the population, the eastern Indian state of Andhra Pradesh was divided into the two states of Telangana and Andhra Pradesh in 2014.

India extends over an area of 3.2 million km² and is the seventh largest territorial state in the world in geographical terms. The country's territory exceeds that of the European Union by over a third. Because of its size and geographical separation from the rest of Asia, India is referred to as a sub-continent. It borders Pakistan to the north-west and China, Myanmar, Nepal and Bangladesh to the north. In rough terms, the country can be divided up into the Himalayas in the north, the Thar Desert in the north-west, and the highlands which cover central and southern India.

India comprises 29 federal states and seven union territories (including the National Capital Territory of Delhi) (see Federal Foreign Office 2015). Union territories are controlled centrally by the government. As India's capital city, Delhi enjoys a special legal status. Further cities of particular importance include Mumbai, Bangalore, Chennai, Kolkata and Pune (see Vermeer/Neumann 2015, p. 16).

Since independence, India has been described as the largest and most populous democracy on earth. During the initial decades following independence, it was dominated by the Congress Party, whose two best-known leadership personalities during the era were arguably Jawaharlal Nehru and Indira Gandhi. In order to obtain a better overview of this situation, the aim below is to provide a brief presentation of the existing political system.

According to its Constitution, India is a secular, democratic and federal republic. Pursuant to the basic principle of separation of powers, the democratic system is divided into executive, legislative and judicial branches (see Federal Foreign Office 2015; bpb 2014a; Debroy/Tellis/Reece 2014; Hardgrave/Kochanek 2008).

At the central state level, the executive is represented by the president, who is chosen by an Election Committee comprising members of the federal and state parliaments. The president appoints the prime minister. The office of president mainly comprises representative tasks, whereas the prime minister stands at the heart of power (see Kooperation International 2014; bpb 2015). India's legislative branch consists of a two-chamber system encompassing a lower house (Lok Sabha) and an upper house (Rajya Sabha). The legislative period is five years, and parliamentary seats are allocated via a first-past-the-post voting system. Following elections, the strongest party has the formal right to nominate the prime minister. Members of the upper house are elected for six years, whereby one third stands for election every two years. Two thirds of members of parliament are determined indirectly by the parliaments of the federal states and by some union territories or via appointment by the president.

The judicial branch is represented by the Supreme Court, whose members are appointed by the president. The Supreme Court comprises 21 high courts, which constitute the highest courts of the states. Because India is made up of 29 federal states, some high courts are responsible for more than one state (see bpb 2014a; Betz 1997; Vermeer/Neumann 2015; Hardgrave/Kochanek 2008).

Political leadership at federal state level is in the hands of a number of governors, who are appointed by the president for a term of five years. The federal states can also create their own parliaments and constitutions. The seven union territories are governed centrally and administered by so-called lieutenant governors (see Vermeer/Neumann 2015, p. 9).

The political and administrative branches try to limit discrimination against minorities. Article 46 of the Constitution of India stipulates particular protection for disadvantaged groups of the population. These particularly include dalits and other lower castes. Positive discrimination quotas exist in the civil service, in the parliaments and in the educational sector (see Lang-Wojtasik 2013, p. 216). Disadvantaged groups are given preferences in areas such as the reservation of jobs in the public sector or the awarding of higher education places. India also has many caste-specific parties which know how to make use of the benefits offered by democracy and attempt to secure privileges for their followers (see bpb 2014b). Overall dialogue in India on the discrimination associated with the castes contains contradictions, and these are explained in Chapter 1.3.

1.3 General economic conditions

Since the early 1990s, India's economic policy has been marked by liberalisation, modernisation and diversification. Reform endeavours undertaken since 1991 have brought huge increases in the economy (see Table 6 and Table 7). An opening up of the economy combined with increasing productivity in all industrial sectors has enabled India to achieve steady growth which only flattened out to around 4 per cent in 2011/2012 (see bpb 2014a; Vermeer/Neumann 2015, p. 49). After a number of years of seeming recession, the 2016 budget year saw India once again record economic growth of 7.6 per cent. This makes it one of the fastest-growing economies in the world (see GTAI 2016). Over the past few years, India has primarily achieved this immense growth via expansion within the services sector (in the fields of company services, banking and telecommuni-cations) and in the industrial sector (in capital-intensive branches) (see Debroy/Tellis/Reece 2014, p. 50). Agriculture accounts for only a marginal proportion of economic performance, and output figures have been falling continuously for a number of years. However, despite its declining significance, the primary sector is still the largest in terms of number of persons employed (see Federal Foreign Office 2015). India's overall em-ployment rate, i.e. the proportion of persons within the population who make up the la-bour supply, is 53.7 per cent (see Destatis 2017). Of these, 49.7 per cent, approximately 21.5 per cent and 28.7 per cent work in the primary, secondary and tertiary sectors, respectively (see Table 9).

Table 6: GDP in India up to 2015 [in billions of US dollars]

Year	GDP
1990	326.61
2000	476.61
2010	1,656.6
2011	1,823
2012	1,829
2013	1,863.2
2014	2,042.4
2015	2,095.4

Source: World Bank 2017c

Table 7: GDP per capita up to 2015 [in US dollars]

Year	GDP per capita
1990	375.15
2000	452.41
2010	1,345.72
2011	1,461.37
2012	1,447.45
2013	1,456.2
2014	1,576.81
2015	1,598.25

Source: World Bank 2017d

Table 8: Proportions of GDP contributed by the economic sectors [in %]

	Agriculture	Industry	Services
1960	42.56	19.30	38.14
1970	41.95	20.48	37.57
1980	35.39	24.29	40.32
1990	29.02	26.49	44.48
2000	23.02	26	50.98
2010	18.88	32.43	48.69
2011	18.53	32.5	48.97
2012	18.25	31.73	50.02
2013	18.33	30.81	50.86
2014	17.39	30.01	52.6
2015	17.05	29.72	53.23

Source: World Bank, year of publication not stated

Table 9: Labour demand by economic sectors in India up to 2013 [in %]

	Agriculture	Industry	Services
2000	59.9	16	24
2005	55.8	19	25.2
2010	51.1	22.4	26.6
2012	47.2	24.7	28.1
2013	49.7	21.5	28.7

Source: World Bank, year of publication not stated

Within an extremely heterogeneous economic structure, there are many branches which are expanding. Examples that may be listed here include infrastructure development in the form of construction of airports, container ports and motorways, and a beacon project to expand the rail link between Mumbai and Delhi, whilst at the same time developing new industrial areas along this route (see Vermeer/Neumann 2015). Major areas of economic growth in the secondary sector include the automobile, chemical and pharmaceutical industries, the textile sector and engineering (see Debroy/Tellis/ Reece 2014, p. 51; Hahn 2005). The services sector also has a major role to play. Aspects such as communications and company-related services (including business outsourcing centres and services in the field of medicine) make up almost 60 per cent of GDP (see Table 8). Information technology and the information technology enabled services sector (IT/ITES sector) and tourism are further branches which are booming (see Debroy/ Tellis/Reece 2014; Vermeer/Neumann 2015).

The labour market is driven by employment in the informal sector. This encompasses family-run and small businesses in agriculture, manufacturing and services and is not controlled or taxed by the state. As a consequence, there are no legally binding regulations within the informal sector. This means that around 90 per cent of all employees in India do not have a formal contract of employment and therefore have no claim to social benefits or old-age provision (see Federal Foreign Office 2015; Singh 1996). According to estimates, around 60 per cent of GDP is produced in this non-organised sector. A study conducted by the Asian Productivity Organisation in 2012 puts India's labour productivity measured against GDP adjusted for purchase power at €3.40 per capita and hour of work. Compared to other Asian countries such as China or Sri Lanka, labour productivity in India is significantly lower (see GTAI 2015).

Despite an immense number of potential workers and a low official unemployment rate, India is facing major challenges in terms of combating poverty and in educational and infrastructure development (see Table 10). Average annual per capita income is €1,100. About 30 per cent of the population live below the poverty threshold of 1 US dollar per person per day. India is in the 135th position of all 187 states included in the United Nations Development Programme (UNDP) Human Development Index (see Federal Foreign Office 2015).

Table 10: Unemployment rate in India up to 2014 [in %][2]

Year	Unemployment rate
2000	4.3
2010	3.5
2011	3.5
2012	3.6
2013	3.6
2014	3.6

Source: World Bank 2017d

In some sectors in particular, India's economic performance is based on a good educational system. One example of this is the successful information technology branch. The overall situation is, however, highly differentiated. Quality in the academic and non-academic sector exhibits considerable variances. India enjoys a good worldwide reputation in academic higher education, particularly via the renowned Indian Institutes of

---

2   The statistics show the unemployment rate without the informal sector. They also represent estimates made by the ILO (International Labour Organization) and for this reason cannot be compared with Western surveys.

Technology (IIT) and Indian Institutes of Management (IIM). By way of contrast, there is a multitude of further state and private universities which are unable to offer training of good quality (see GTAI 2015). Many companies complain of insufficient relevance to practice and of the failure of academic training to deliver skills. Against this background, companies state that they often rely on company-based induction or "training on the job" (see Mehrotra 2014; Zenner/Pilz 2015). The main focus in the non-academic sector is on the shortage of workers who have completed technical training, particularly in the traditional craft trade occupations (see GTAI 2015).

In the field of vocational education and training, there are both state and private sector training centres [Industrial Training Institutes] (ITI) as well as colleges (for more detailed information see Chapters 4.3.1 to 5.4.1). Lack of relevance to practice is also an object of complaint in this regard, as are a poor infrastructure, obsolete curricula and the quality of training given to trainers. Another point of criticism is the absence of cooperation with companies providing training (see Mehrotra 2014; GTAI 2015). High drop-out rates and unemployment following qualification are also criticised (see Pilz et al. 2015a). All of these aspects are discussed in detail in Chapters 4.1 and 5.6.

2 Typical vocational education and training processes or training programmes

This chapter outlines three fictitious curricula vitae, each of which represents an example of typical training processes in India. The institutions and education and training programmes mentioned in the curricula vitae will be explained accordingly in the following chapters.

2.1 Learning in the informal sector

Tutan is 20 years old and works as a fisherman in a small village on the coast of the State of Odisha in the Bay of Bengal. He lives with his parents and six siblings and will shortly marry a girl from a neighbouring village. Tutan attended the state-run village school until Year Five. As the eldest child, however, he then had to leave school in order to help his father in his fishing business on a daily basis. He is proud that he will soon be able to start his own family, as earnings from fish sales have risen over recent years. One reason for this is that, over the years, Tutan's father has taught his son everything he needs to know about catching fish. Tutan is able to steer the small boat and knows the best fishing grounds. He can identify fish diseases and species. He looks after the equipment and is familiar with the best ways of preserving fish in the heat. Another reason why he is able to get by is a new service introduced by the local fishery cooperative a few months ago. Every day, Tutan receives texts on his mobile phone informing him of the latest wholesale fish prices. Since this time, he has been able to obtain significantly better prices from the fish wholesalers. Tutan is confident that the situation will continue to improve in future because of an initiative launched by the regional government to prevent overfishing and pollution of this particular stretch of coastline. Nevertheless, Tutan would like his children to pursue a different occupation in the nearest large town. Perhaps they could work as office messengers or housekeepers.

2.2 Training at a small craft trade company

Muthu is 22. He is single and lives on the outskirts of New Delhi. He is originally from the South of India, where his family still lives. In his home town, he attended secondary school until the end of Year Nine. After this, his family allowed him to attend an ITI, where he spent two years learning the basic principles of bicycle and motorcycle mechanics. Although Muthu enjoyed this period very much because he could still live with his family without having to help out in the household all the time like his younger sister, there is one aspect of the training that he regrets when he looks back today. He attended many hours of teaching, but these were often tedious. Teachers gave long lectures, and there was seldom an opportunity to carry out real work on components or to be involved in the practical maintenance of bicycles or motorcycles. Because the local prospects of employment were extremely poor upon completion of this training, a distant uncle from New Delhi helped Muthu to get a job within the metropolitan area of the city in a bicycle and motorcycle mechanics workshop with eight employees. In this workshop, Muthu was then taught the practical side of his trade. Every day, he learned by observing the other workers and also received instruction from his boss. Now, four years later, a great opportunity has opened up for him. Because his employment in the workshop is not subject to any statutory regulations, he can be given notice at any time. The wages he receives are also far from munificent. Now Muthu would like to open his own workshop. He believes that this is his only chance to be an attractive prospect as a bridegroom whilst continuing to support his family at the same time. His father is no longer able to work following a road traffic accident, and medical treatment remains a very costly factor. After training as a nurse in Kerala, his older sister has a well-paid job in an Arabian country. She has said that she will lend him the money to start his own business. Muthu is full of expectation for the future.

2.3 Academic education as the "gold standard"

25-year old Usha is just about to move to Bangalore. She has received an attractive job offer from a major Indian IT company there and indeed had plenty of other offers to choose from. Usha comes from Chennai, where her parents and a younger brother still live. Her father has a degree and works as an engineer for a government authority. Her mother is a doctor at a children's hospital. Usha attended a private secondary school in Chennai. As a young girl, however, she did not apply herself to her studies and her parents were disappointed with her school results. They insisted that she move to a Christian boarding school in the Nilgiri Hills in the East of the state of Tamil Nadu. Once there, she suffered frequently from homesickness and everyday school life was very strict. But these deprivations and the high school fees were worthwhile in the end. Usha completed her upper secondary certificate. Because she was interested in computers, her father recommended that she should attend a respected private university in Vellore, in the centre of the state. Because the marks she had achieved at school were modest, her family had to buy a study place. Together with the high fees charged, this represented a further considerable investment. However, this once again paid off, as Usha found her fulfilment by studying for a Bachelor degree in information technology. In her final year, she achieved the best marks of any female student and successfully applied to study for a Master's degree at the Indian Institute of Technology Madras (in Chennai). She was able to expand her competencies further and even spent a year studying abroad. She now has a qualification that opens up all the doors. In Bangalore, she hopes to pursue a career and make good progress in her chosen profession. She is not yet thinking about starting a family. Her primary focus at the moment is on her working life.

3 Overview of the educational system

Basic data

Table 11: Pupils and students by educational sectors [in thousands]

Level	Pupils and students
Primary (I–V)	130,501
Upper primary (VI–VIII)	67,165
Elementary (I–VIII)	197,666
Secondary (IX–X)	38,301
Senior secondary (XI–XII)	235,967
PhD	118
MPhil	33
Postgraduate	3,853
Undergraduate	27,172
PG Diploma	215
Diploma	2,508
Certificate	170
Integrated	142
Higher education total	34,211

Source: MHRD 2016d

Table 12: Enrolment by educational sectors and age groups [in 100,000s]

Level/year	Primary	Upper primary	Secondary	Higher secondary	Higher education
1950–51	192	31	N/A	15	4
1960–61	350	67	N/A	34	10
1970–71	570	133	N/A	76	33
1980–81	738	207	N/A	110	48
2000–01	1,138	428	190	99	86
2005–06	1,321	522	250	134	143
2006–07	1,337	545	259	141	156
2007–08	1,355	573	282	163	172
2008–09	1,353	584	294	169	185
2009–10	1,336	595	307	178	207
2010–11	1,347	619	318	195	275
2011–12	1,398	630	341	210	292
2012–13 (P)	1,348	650	346	200	301
2013–14 (P)	1,324	664	373	223	323
2014–15 (P)	1,305	672	383	235	342

P = provisional, N/A = not available
Source: MHRD 2016d

Table 13: Number of pupils per teacher by educational sectors

Type of educational establishment	Number of teachers	Number of pupils per teacher
Primary	2,670,396	24
Upper primary	2,559,769	17
Secondary	1,346,888	27
Senior secondary	1,984,711	38
Higher education	1,319,295	24

Source: MHRD 2016

Table 14: Number of pupils per teacher by educational sectors and years

Level/year	Primary	Upper primary	Secondary	Higher secondary	Higher education
1950–51	24	30	N/A	21	N/A
1960–61	36	31	N/A	25	N/A
1970–71	39	32	N/A	25	N/A
1980–81	38	33	N/A	27	N/A
1990–91	43	37	N/A	31	N/A
2000–01	43	38	31	35	N/A
2005–06	46	34	32	34	26
2006–07	44	34	31	34	N/A
2007–08	47	35	33	37	20
2008–09	45	34	32	38	21
2009–10	41	33	30	39	24
2010–11	43	33	30	34	26
2011–12	41	34	32	33	24
2012–13 (P)	28	25	N/A	N/A	23
2013–14 (P)	25	17	26	41	25
2014–15 (P)	24	17	27	38	24

P = provisional; N/A = not available
Source: MHRD 2016

Table 15: Number of teachers by educational sectors [in 1,000s]

Level/year	Primary	Upper primary	Secondary	Higher secondary
1950–51	538	86	N/A	127
1960–61	742	345	N/A	296
1970–71	1,060	638	N/A	629
1980–81	1,363	851	N/A	926
1990–91	1,616	1,073	N/A	1,334
2000–01	1,896	1,326	1,006	756
2005–06	2,184	1,671	1,123	1,032
2006–07	2,323	1,717	1,173	1,075
2007–08	2,315	1,780	1,175	952
2008–09	2,229	1,899	1,194	1,024
2009–10	2,217	1,778	1,185	1,145
2010–11	2,099	1,887	1,247	1,261
2011–12	2,254	2,057	1,163	1,303
2012–13 (P)	2,656	2,427	944	1,799
2013–14 (P)	2,684	2,513	1,286	1,785
2014–15 (P)	2,670	2,560	1,347	1,985

P = provisional, N/A = not available
Source: MHRD 2016

Table 16: Drop-out rates by educational sectors

Classes/year	Classes I–V	Classes I–VIII	Classes I–X
1960–61	64.9	78.3	N/A
1970–71	67.0	77.9	N/A
1980–81	58.7	72.7	82.5
1990–91	42.6	60.9	71.3
2000–01	40.7	53.7	68.6
2005–06	25.7	48.8	61.6
2006–07	25.6	45.9	59.9
2007–08	25.1	42.7	56.7
2008–09	27.8	39.3	54.2
2009–10	30.3	42.5	52.7
2010–11	27.4	40.8	49.2
2011–12	22.3	40.8	50.3
2012–13 (P)	21.3	39.0	50.4
2013–14 (P)	19.8	36.3	47.4

P = provisional, N/A = not available
Source: MHRD 2014

3.1 Historic origins and the status quo

The history of education and teaching in India has its beginnings in educational establishments at Hindu temples (1000 BC), in which an elite circle received training from
gurukuls (guru/teacher). Over a long period of time, religious influences left their mark
on Indian education. These included education in Buddhist monasteries, educational
establishments connected with Islam (maktabs and madrasahs), institutes associated
with other religions (e.g. Jains, Sikhs) as well as Christian schools (see Lang-Wojtasik
2014, pp. 216 ff.).

More recent educational developments, particularly in the higher education sector,
have been influenced by British colonial rule. After independence in 1947, the Indian
educational system continued to be characterised by its original 10+2 structure, and
this was recognised by all states and union territories at a national level. The 10+2 system is divided into ten years of basic education followed by two years of optional higher
secondary education (see Chapter 3.4.4).

3.2 Control

In political terms, the educational sector in India is established at multiple layers. As
the lead authority responsible, the Ministry of Human Resources Development (MHRD)
assumes an important and influential position. The MHRD is divided into two depart-
ments: the Department of School Education and Literacy and the Department of Higher
Education. The MHRD is supported by the All India Council for Technical Education
(AICTE) (see Chapter 5.2) in the administration of the vocational education and training system, in particular via the accreditation of programmes of study at technical colleges and polytechnics (see Männicke 2011; Kooperation International 2015). Beside
the AICTE, which is responsible for technical higher education, there is also the University Grants Commission (UGC), which stipulates and manages higher education standards. As well as including regulation of internal higher education task areas, the remit
of the UGC also encompasses the further key area of recognition of Indian universities
(see Chapter 3.4.5).

The ministry is managed by the Central Board of Education (CABE), which controls
the task areas of the central and state governments. The Board of the CABE is made
up by ministers from the various federal states. The National Council of Educational
Research and Training (NCERT) is responsible at national level for the definition of
general conditions for classes one to twelve (curriculum development). The respective
State Councils of Education Research and Training (SCERT) form the most important
research and development institutions at regional level (Norric 2006).

In the secondary sector, the school authorities are responsible at state level for communication and links between schools and for the stipulation of examination stand-

ards in accordance with national general conditions (see Kooperation International 2015). The three national examination boards are the Central Board of Secondary Education (CBSE),[3] the Council for the Indian School Certificate Examinations (CISCE)[4] (see Chapter 3.4.4) and the National Institute for Open Schooling (NIOS) (see Chapter 3.4.8). Each state also has its own respective "State Educational Board" (see Cheney et al. 2005).

3.3 Structure

Mandatory schooling and the right to receive a school place free of charge for children aged between six and 14 was introduced in the Constitution of India in 2009 (Right to Free and Compulsory Education Act 2009). Following optional pre-school provision, access of children to the general educational system begins with eight years of elementary education, which in India is divided into primary (classes 1 to 5) and upper primary education (classes 6 to 8). After completion of elementary education, there is the possibility of entering general secondary education (classes 9 and 10) and then higher secondary education (classes 11 and 12). The latter may be academically or vocationally oriented. Tertiary education is offered at colleges and universities (see Lang-Wojtasik 2013).

The Indian educational system exhibits various organisational forms. Some states have government school systems (e.g. Bihar, Jharkhand, Punjab und Himachal Pradesh), others are privately organised with state support (private aided) (e.g. West Bengal, Maharashtra, Gujarat) whilst some are private and self-financed (private unaided) (e.g. Uttar Pradesh, Tamil Nadu, Rajasthan). This means that any comparison between federal states regarding cost-benefit ratios or school performance is virtually impossible (see World Bank 2008, p. xxii).

Since 2014, school enrolment rates have been rising in the private sector in particular. By way of contrast, there are high drop-out rates in the state primary sector. Drop-out rates (all categories)[5] in the primary sector (classes 1 to 8) are 36.3 per cent. The corresponding figure for the primary and secondary sectors in overall terms (classes 1 to 10) is 47.4 per cent (school year 2013/14) (see MHRD 2014, p. 43). There are many reasons why a child may drop out of education whilst still at primary school. These include migration of families, child marriage or child labour, and inadequate school infrastructure (drinking water and toilets).

These educational programmes within the formal sector are localised under the umbrella of the National Vocational Education Qualifications Framework (NVEQF). The National Qualifications Framework was developed in 2011 in order to align and document qualifications at all formal educational levels within a uniform system encompass-

---

3   Schools affiliated to the CBSE take part in the All India Secondary School Examination (AISSE).

4   Schools affiliated to the CISCE take part in the Indian Certificate of Secondary Education (ICSE).

5   Scheduled Caste, Scheduled Tribe, Rural, Urban.

ing school education, VET and higher education (levels 1–10, Table 17). The NVEQF should be read as a sequence of various competencies, beginning with the recognition of prior qualifications designated in Table 17 as RPL 1 and RPL 2 (see Chapter 5.6.2). Formal qualifications are legible on the basis of levels one to ten. The various levels are defined by learning performance, i.e. they list the competencies which a learner needs to have mastered irrespective of whether these have been achieved by formal or informal means (see Singh/Duvekot 2013, pp.109 ff.; Singh 2017).

Table 17: Structure of the NVEQF

Level	Certificate	Vocational education Equivalence	Academic education Equivalence	Certifying body
10	NCC 8	Degree	Doctorate	University and SCC
9	NCC 7	PG Diploma	Master's	University and SCC
8	NCC 6			University and SCC
7	NCC 5	Advanced Diploma*	Bachelor degree**	*Technical education committee and SSC **University and SCC
6	NCC 4			
5	NCC 3	Diploma*		*Technical education committee and SSC **School board and SSC
4	NCC 2		Class XII**	
3	NCC 1		Class XI**	
2	NCWP 2	Class X	Class X	School board and SSC
1	NCWP 1	Class IX	Class IX	School board and SSC
RPL	RPL 2	Class VIII	Class VIII	NIOS/State Open School and SSC
	RPL 1	Class V	Class V	NIOS/State Open School and SSC

RPL: Recognition of Prior Learning
NCWP: National Certificate for Work Preparation
NCC: National Competency Certificate
SSC: Sector Skill Council
Source: MHRD 2012

3.4 Characterisation of the various educational sectors

3.4.1 Pre-school

Pre-school education in India is optional and varies in length between two and three years (see Norric 2006). In urban regions, pre-schools are largely privately organised and well developed. This means that pre-school education is available to a large proportion of better-off pupils. In rural areas, by way of contrast, pre-school education tends to be publicly provided and, according to the National Policy on Education (NPE), needs to be expanded further (well-trained teachers, provision of free meals, and a safe and healthy learning environment (see Lang-Wojtasik 2013, p. 218).

There are anganwadis [childcare centres], which are centrally financed, and balwadis [pre-schools],[6] which are funded by the federal state or local government. Anganwadis are the largest educational provider in this sector, and these institutions are currently attended by over twelve million children aged between three and six. Both anganwadis and balwadis place their emphasis on under-privileged groups in rural regions. Crèches or day centres are financed by the public Central Social Welfare Board. Early years education is also delivered by NGOs and many private institutions, such as crèches, nursery schools, or via part-time provision at private schools (see Chandra 2003, p. 10; Gupta 2007, p. 93).

3.4.2 Primary sector [primary/upper primary education]

Elementary education is divided into primary school (classes 1 to 5) and upper primary school (classes 6 to 8). In the primary sector, there is a differentiation between state, semi-state and private schools. A further distinction may be drawn between schools in rural areas, whose pupils are often socially disadvantaged, and schools in affluent urban regions (see Lang-Wojtasik 2014, p. 219).

As a consequence of the diversity within the primary education sector, the Right to Free and Compulsory Education Act 2009 also stipulated that private schools must reserve at least a quarter of their places for pupils from socially disadvantaged families or for children with a disability. All federal states were required to enable every child to go to school within three years of enactment of the legislation by establishing new neighbourhood schools in regions where supply is inadequate. Parents or employers who prevent children from attending school may be subject to a fine (www.mhrd.gov.in).

According to a national study conducted by Pratham (2015), state schools have made enormous progress with regard to equipment. The main object of criticism in recent years has been the inadequate nature of sanitary facilities. These have seen signifi-

---

6   Anganwadis and balwadis are part of a state-instigated programme to combat malnutrition of children and form part of the Integrated Child Development Services (ICDS) initiated by UNICEF.

cant improvement within the space of four years. Whereas in 2010 toilets and wash basins were only available in 47.2 per cent of cases, this figure rose to 65.2 per cent by 2014. Supply of drinking water also improved by 2.9 percentage points during this period. In 2010, freely accessible libraries were available in 62.6 per cent of schools. By 2014, this accessibility had increased to 78.1 per cent.

There are, however, also points of weakness in the system. Of all the children attending Year Five, 50 per cent remain under the stipulated reading level for Year Two. The figures relating to mathematical knowledge are also a cause of concern. The number of children in Years Two and Three who are unable to count to nine has risen over the course of the years. The number of pupils with inadequate knowledge of numbers increased from 11.3 per cent in 2009 to 19.5 per cent in 2014 (Pratham 2015).

There are high drop-out rates in the primary sector. To put these in figures: 29 per cent of children left elementary education after completion of primary school or by the end of Year Five (between ten and eleven, many children enter the age at which they are deployed as child labourers). Forty-three per cent of children leave education after finishing upper primary school. This makes India one of the five nations in the world with the highest rate of non-attendance of elementary education. 1.4 million children aged between six and eleven do not go to school (see Sahni 2015).

3.4.3 Secondary education

At the end of mandatory schooling, i.e. at the age of 14, children can make the transition to the two-year lower secondary sector (class 9 and 10). Teaching takes place at general schools that are attended by more than 36 million pupils. The prerequisite for entry is completion of upper primary school (class 8). A fee based on the financial means of the parents is charged for education in classes 9 and 10. Families with the lowest level of income are required to pay fees in the amount of INR 500. This figure rises to INR 6,800 for pupils from the wealthiest families (MHRD 2016f, p.8).

Close cooperation takes place between the schools and central government and individual federal state authorities (see MHRD 2014). The national curriculum contains a total of eight subjects to be taught in the general education sector. In specific terms, the teaching of the following subjects is obligatory at all schools: two to three languages, including mother tongue/regional language, Hindi and/or English (a few schools also offer other languages such as Sanskrit, Chinese, Japanese, Russian, French, Spanish, Arabic, Persian or German), three elective subjects such as mathematics, music or graphic design, general studies, work experience and health education (CBSE 2015, p. 37) (see Table 18).

Table 18: Selection of teaching subjects, general secondary education

Subject
Language I
Language II
Three elective subjects from a total of 32 offered[7]
Work education or pre-vocational training
Art education
Health education

Source: CBSE 2015, p. 37

The national curriculum for the pre-vocational sector in classes 9 and 10 comprises a total of eight subjects, and pupils can select both general and vocational subjects. They are able to choose from 32 elective subjects in the general area and from 40 elective subjects on the vocational side (see Table 19). Only selected schools offer these courses, and such schools need to be recognised by the CBSE (Tara/Kumar 2016).

Table 19: Selection of teaching subjects, pre-vocational secondary education

Subject
Language I (English)
Two subjects from general secondary education
Two elective subjects from 40 possible vocational courses[8]
One additional subject from a choice of general or vocational subjects
Work-integrated learning
Personal development and soft skills
Total

Source: CBSE 2015, pp. 38 ff.

Evaluation of performance takes place on the basis of a continuous procedure which is stipulated by the central government or federal state school authority. Final exami-

---

7   Mathematics, Physics, Chemistry, Biology, Biotechnology, Engineering Graphics, Economics, Political Science, History, Geography, Business Studies, Accountancy, Home Science, Fine Arts, Agriculture, Computer Science/Informatics Practices, Multimedia and Web Technology, Sociology, Psychology, Philosophy, Physical Education, Music and Dance, Entrepreneurship, Fashion Studies, Creative Writing and Translation Studies, Heritage Crafts, Graphic Design, Mass Media Studies and Knowledge Traditions and Practices of India, Legal Studies, Human Rights and Gender Studies and National Cadet Corps.

8   Including Office Secretaryship, Stenography and Computer Applications, Accountancy and Auditing, Marketing and Salesmanship, Banking, Retail, Business Administration etc.

nations in India are held at the end of class 10 in the form of the All India Secondary School Certificate (AISSC), the Indian Certificate of Secondary Education (ICSE) or the Secondary School Certificate (SSC). In the ICSE, for example, pupils are examined in six subjects. Pupils are required to achieve a pass in at least five of the six subjects in order to gain access to the upper secondary sector. English is compulsory, and there are five further elective subjects.

A direct comparison initiated by the British Council indicated that the Indian Secondary School Certificate (which is awarded by every school upon completion of Year Ten) lies below the educational standard of the British General Certificate of Secondary Education (GCSE) or the GCSE High School Examination Certificate, which is awarded internationally. Although the content is comparable, the level of problem-solving competence and application of knowledge, for example, does not meet the relatively high British standard (see Cheney et al. 2005, p. 8).

According to the statistics (see Table 16), most pupils leave general schooling at the end of class 10 when they are aged 15 or 16. Reasons for this include financial constraints, a lack of interest in lessons, qualification is sufficient for further career progression or direct transition to the labour market (Ahir 2015).

3.4.4 Higher secondary education

The upper secondary sector encompasses classes 11 and 12. In order to complete higher secondary education, pupils may attend a secondary school or junior college. Although the junior college is affiliated to universities, it is categorised as a pre-university educational establishment. India has more than 200,000 secondary schools, which are attended by in excess of 23.5 million pupils (see MHRD 2016d). The prerequisite for transition to the upper secondary sector is performance in the final examinations at the end of the tenth year of schooling (see Cheney et al. 2005; Sodhi 2014).

Higher secondary education is an important stage for pupils within the educational system. Prior to entering the higher secondary level, they have to decide on their future educational pathway. The choice is between preparation for higher education, technical training or direct entry to the labour market (see Planning Commission 2013).

Pre-vocational training aimed at preparing pupils for the world of work may form an essential component of secondary education. Pre-vocational training is part of the official curriculum and runs parallel to general education (Krisanthan/Pilz 2014). Admission to the upper secondary sector entitles pupils to choose between two options. They can elect to pursue an academic (technical) or a vocational pathway. The aim of the academic route is seen as preparation for a further professional career. The vocational pathway prepares pupils for direct entry to the labour market upon completion of class 11 or 12 (Gupta et al. 2006).

The MSDE offers an additional programme at numerous state ITIs and private ITIs in order to provide training for young people, women and disadvantaged groups (for detailed information, see Chapter 4.3.1).

After completion of general upper secondary education, pupils are able to obtain the All India Senior School Certificate. This facilitates entry to higher education.

3.4.5 Higher education

Currently (as of 2016), India has 760 institutions which offer academic programmes of study. These include 316 state universities, 181 state private universities, 122 deemed-to-be-universities, 75 institutions of national importance (Indian Institutes of Technology (IITs), national institutes of technology (NITs), Indian Institutes of Science Education and Research (IISERs) and further institutions (see MHRD 2016d). "Deemed-to-be-universities" are frequently private universities that have been certified by the state.

In turn, the universities consist of a series of colleges at which teaching takes place. Over the past few years, the number of colleges has multiplied to reach 38,498 institutions by the year 2015 (MHRD 2016d). Colleges can be differentiated by degree of autonomy, nature of provider and financing. Providers are either the state or the private sector, although the colleges either belong to a university or else are subject to the respective federal state government. Most courses offered by the colleges are "undergraduate" programmes. Development of curricula, implementation of final examinations and awarding of academic qualifications from the programmes take place via the university (see Hahn 2005, p. 35).

According to enrolment rates, India is the third largest provider of academic programmes after China and the USA. The number of students is currently around 30 million. According to the Department for Higher Education, the aim is to raise this figure to over 40 million by 2020.

Access to higher education is controlled. In general terms, the following access options exist in India. The best students are accepted after an entrance examination (Merit List). Pupils or their families may also purchase a study place at a fixed fee (capitation fee), and reserved quotas exist for disadvantaged population groups (see Hahn 2005, p. 39). The basic prerequisite for access is the result achieved in the Higher Secondary School Certificate (HSSC). Depending on the institution, higher education applicants must also prepare themselves for an entrance test (All India Entrance Test) or an interview. The best Indian students strive to be accepted by one of the top institutions. The high degree of esteem accorded to academic education within Indian society means that completion of a programme of higher education study guarantees secure employment (see Wessels 2012).

As already summarised in Chapter 3.2, responsibilities for higher education rest with the MHRD, the AICTE and the UGC. Despite the strong influence exerted by the state institutions, universities largely enjoy autonomy in the awarding of academic degrees as well as in the area of research. A differentiation is made between public and private institutions with full university status which offer the whole spectrum of subject combinations on the one hand and specialised universities only providing certain subject areas on the other. "Institutes of National Importance" is a term applied to elite universities which have been designated as institutes of higher education by the government and thus have the right to award their own degrees. These include higher education establishments such as the IITs or the Indian Institutes of Management (IIMs), which occupy top positions in international higher education ranking systems (see Hahn 2005). "Deemed-to-be-universities" are high-performing institutions which have been established by the central government upon recommendation of the UCG.

This multi-layered higher education system is aligned to the qualifications of Bachelor, Masters and PhD in accordance with British standards. In addition, there are graduate and postgraduate diploma programmes.

Bachelor degree programmes in the humanities, the sciences and economic sciences comprise a three-year course of study. In other disciplines, duration of the programme of study may vary. A Bachelor programme may, for example, extend over a period of four years if students elect to study agricultural science, engineering, dentistry or veterinary medicine. Programmes in architecture or human medicine may be of up to five years in duration.

A Bachelor degree is the prerequisite for entry to a Master's programme of study. A Master's degree can usually be achieved following a course-based or research-based period of study of two years (see Cheney et al. 2005; Norric 2006). The highest possible qualification, only offered by some universities, is a PhD. The PhD is a two-year doctorate programme which requires previous completion of a Master's degree. The doctorate itself can be acquired following completion of the PhD programme and of a thesis and is achieved over varying periods of time (usually four or five years) (see Hahn 2005, pp. 33 ff.).

India is undergoing a phenomenon known as "massification". Massification refers to the process of a growing society in certain areas. Clearly discernible trends in this regard are occurring in the field of higher education. These include an increase in the number of institutions, rising enrolment rates, and the increasing privatisation (commercialisation) and professionalisation of university institutions (see Khare 2016, p. 121; Hahn 2005).

3.4.6 Post-secondary education

Polytechnics

Students can opt for full-time or part-time courses. The minimum requirement for entry to the programme is completion of class ten and completion of class 12 for certain selected courses. Polytechnics offer sub-degree diploma courses of a duration of between one and three years. There are, however, also three- to four-year diploma courses and one-year postgraduate diploma courses. The postgraduate programmes are aimed at persons who are already in possession of a polytechnic diploma or Bachelor degree. Training is primarily theoretical in nature and is delivered at polytechnic colleges. Some units are, however, of a practical nature (Norric 2006). Students can normally choose between six possible occupational fields. These are agriculture, business, metalworking and electrotechnology, health, housekeeping and services (Wessels 2012). The stipulation of standards and evaluation of the programme is undertaken by the State Boards of Technical Education. Titles, duration and access qualifications vary from state to state. This means that particular care needs to be taken when enrolling (Norric 2006). Polytechnics are generally recognised by the AICTE (MHRD 2016e).

Those completing the polytechnic programmes are able to offer specific skills such as the reading and interpretation of drawings, cost calculation and repair and maintenance of machines. For this reason, many small and medium-sized companies are particularly interested in employing such persons once they have obtained their qualification (Khare 2016; Goel 2009).

Today there is a total of 3,867 institutions with 1,515,597 enrolments (All India Survey on Higher Education 2015-2016 (MHRD 2016e, p. 35). The intention is also to establish a further 700 institutions under the MHRD Skill Development Initiative. Of these, the plan is for 300 to be initiated via partnerships under public law. In detailed terms, this will involve cooperation between the state governments/union territories in agreement with the Confederation of Indian Industry (CII), the Federation of Indian Chambers of Commerce & Industry (FICCI), the Associated Chambers of Commerce and Industry of India (ASSOCHAM) and the PHD Chamber of Commerce. A further 400 institutions will be run by private providers (see Planning Commission 2013, p. 144).

In comparison to other forms of training provision (CTS, engineering colleges), the polytechnics offer only a small number of training places. For this reason, the AICTE has lowered the regulations regarding the establishment of a new institution and the requirements for accreditation (see Mond/Pilz 2011).

Alongside the state polytechnics, there are also private institutions. Because of the comparatively high costs of the respective courses and the poor quality of teaching and infrastructure, these private institutions are not accredited by the AICTE and are only of very small significance in quantitative terms in technical vocational education and training (see Männicke 2011).

Engineering colleges

Engineering colleges offer vocationally-related higher education. The Undergraduate Degree (UG) Programme provides an opportunity for those who have completed a course of study at a polytechnic to go on to further technical training. Such students have the possibility of entering training at the engineering colleges in the second year (Venkatram 2016, p. 83).

A distinction can be drawn between independent colleges and institutions which are affiliated to universities. This delineation is frequently not clear. In formal terms, the colleges are subject to the AICTE rather than to the UGC, the latter being responsible for university education (see Mond/Pilz 2011, p. 9). There is a total of 5,672 engineering colleges (see Badrinath 2016, p. 234).

3.4.7 Adult and continuing education

State, private and not-for-profit institutions all play a major role in continuing vocational education and training. India has various vocational training programmes in which the borders between initial and continuing VET are fluid. Continuing training programmes tend to be found within the sector of vocational education and training. For this reason, a precise description of continuing vocational education and training will be provided in Chapters 4 and 5.

There is a state-imposed programme, the National Literacy Mission (NLM), which was initiated in 1988 by the Directorate of Adult Education (MHRD, see Chapter 3.2) and places the emphasis on continuing training. This programme is aimed at all those who have been unable to avail themselves of the option of formal education but still wish to pursue continuing training. The designation "Literacy" is somewhat misleading since the development of occupational skills also plays an equally important role (www.mhrd.gov.in). In 1996, Continuing Education Centres (CEC) were established with the goal of equipping venues to improve people's reading and writing skills and thus enhance their quality of life. Alongside this, further development programmes are also in place such as provision of books in specially equipped libraries and the offering of cultural and leisure activities (see Singh 2002).

3.4.8 Open and distance learning

The NIOS was set up as an autonomous organisation by the MHRD in 1989 (NIOS year of publication not stated). The programme has around 2.7 million pupils and is one of the largest of its type anywhere in the world. In the area of elementary education, there are Open Basic Education Programmes (OBE), which are offered in around 853 Accredited Agencies (AA). The NIOS itself is responsible for education in the area of open and distance learning for the lower and upper secondary levels and comprises a network of more than 4,900 study centres (general education 3,530 and vocational education 1,379). These are under the control of 20 regional centres. As well as the general educational programmes, numerous vocational courses are also provided, and these will be described in greater detail in Chapter 5 (NIOS year of publication not stated). The target groups comprise economically and socially disadvantaged groups and school drop-outs. The aim is that these persons should be reintegrated into the public educational system via modular programmes (see World Bank 2009). The NIOS exhibits a number of special characteristics compared to conventional educational programmes. These include a flexible selection of subjects, online admission procedures, multiple repetitions of courses (nine times within five years), support via so-called Personal Contact Programmes (PCP), the possibility of credit transfer and a broad range of media programmes (radio, television, online media). At lower secondary level, there are 26 courses which offer learning materials in various languages such as Hindi, English, Urdu, Marathi, Telugu, Gujarati and Malayalam. Provision at upper secondary level is reduced to a choice of 24 courses in three languages (Hindi, English and Urdu). Any questions which pupils may have can be formulated in any language and receive a response from the study centre in one of the languages listed above regardless of type of school (see NIOS year of publication not stated; World Bank 2009). Final examinations are held twice a year at the respective study centres. Candidates have a free choice of the number of subjects in which they wish to sit an examination. Once the credits stipulated for the respective module have been achieved, the formal criteria for the qualification are deemed to have been fulfilled and a certificate is awarded (see Norric 2006). This programme is partially financed via study fees (usually €4.00–€4.50 per course[9]), although the amount of such fees may vary depending on the institution and pupil. Deficits are covered by financial support from the central government (NIOS year of publication not stated).

Over the course of the years, the programme has achieved a high degree of acceptance and credibility both within formal training and on the labour market. It facilitates the chance of continuing training or finding a job and thus provides better labour market opportunities (see World Bank 2009).

---

9   The exchange rate used for all conversions in this country study is 1 euro = 75 rupees.

4 Initial and continuing vocational education and training

4.1 Development and significance of vocational education and training

The Indian system of vocational education and training (VET) and technical vocational education and training (TVET) is highly diverse regarding form, function and areas of responsibility (Sodhi 2014; British Council 2016).

Education is traditionally accorded great status in India. The caste system is of particular relevance within this context (see Clemens/Holzwarth 2009). Despite its abolition by state ordinance, this system continues to exert a strong influence on Indian society and therefore also on the reputation of the educational system (see Männicke 2011).[10] Parents from higher levels of society enable their children to access higher general education, which is often extremely costly. By way of contrast, the remaining parts of the population are only able to participate in VET or else are completely excluded from educational provision after the end of mandatory schooling. A negative selection process also occurs no later than at the beginning of upper secondary level. Pupils who cannot progress to a higher secondary school because of poor performance are particularly likely to opt for practical training. This gives rise to the impression that vocational education and training is only of interest to young people who have virtually no chance of establishing themselves on the general educational market because of poor marks in final examinations (see World Bank 2008, p.13). Majumdar describes this phenomenon in the following terms.

> "TVET in India is often seen as second-class education and as the last recourse for those who are unable to succeed in academic learning. [...] Aspirations toward higher education and *white collar jobs* and the low perception of VET make TVET attractive only for low academic achievers and for students from low-income families." (Majumdar 2008, p. 96)

According to a survey conducted by the National Sample Survey Organisation (NSSO), only about 3.07 per cent of the population aged between 15 and 59 have completed a programme of vocational training or are currently involved in vocational education and training provision (see Ahmed 2016, p. 333). Mehrotra summarises the low level of participation in the VET system by commenting: "India is among the countries with the lowest proportion of trained youth in the world" (Mehrotra et al. 2014, p. 8). As a consequence, large parts of the population are learning and working within the non-organised or informal sector (see Chapter 4.6).

---

10 The curriculum vitae described above also once again provide a very clear reflection of the indirect effect of the caste system (see Chapter 2).

Beside the low level of participation in VET programmes, many studies and surveys (ILO 2003; World Bank 2008; Mehrotra 2014) criticise the lack of practical relevance in vocational training.

The poor infrastructure, obsolete learning methods and teaching staff who in some cases are badly trained are all further influencing factors which deter young people from entering vocational training (see Mehrotra et al. 2014).

The contrast between the low level of esteem in which practice-related VET is held and the high status enjoyed by general education is also reflected in another way in the employment system. The terms "white-collar worker" and "blue-collar worker" are clearly delineated within the Indian world of work. White-collar workers are considered to be engineers, architects, lawyers and all those who are not required to carry out manual work. Their employment is seen as intellectually challenging and enjoys societal acceptance. All those who fall into the category of blue-collar workers are persons who perform physical tasks and are often employed in industry or manufacturing (see Wessels/Pilz 2016).

The structuring and status of the individual training programmes will be explained in more detail in the following sub-chapters.

4.2 Structure of vocational education and training and provision

Vocational education in the form of the vocational training system is taught in a practically oriented way at independent institutions such as vocational schools. It includes formal VET delivered at state and private Industrial Training Institutes (ITIs) under the Craftsmen Training Scheme (CTS). Alongside these school-based training schemes, there are also formal company-based programmes usually designated as an Apprenticeship Training Scheme (ATS). In-company training, via which participants are able to learn further skills in a practice-related way, is also possible within the scope of an existing contract of employment.

The state-funded Vocationalisation of Secondary Education programme was set up in 1988 in order to balance out the inequality between supply and demand on the labour market. It represents an alternative to the original general pathway in the form of higher education (MHRD 2016a). One hundred fifty different vocational courses are offered in the upper secondary sector. According to the Planning Commission, there are 9,583 participating schools with more than one million pupils. Courses are provided in the fields of agriculture, trade and industry, technology, healthcare and science and engineering (see Gupta et al. 2016, p. 45).

As well as the vocational training system, there is also a pre-vocational education system which is taught at general schools alongside regular lessons in a non-practice-related way ("vocational education"). A distinction can be drawn between the formal secondary sector in the form of pre-vocational and general education in classes 9 and 10 and the higher formal secondary sector in classes 11 and 12.

The Constitution of India stipulates that the central and state governments should share the areas of responsibility in vocational education and training. Vocational education falls within the remit of the MHRD. Responsibility at a central level is borne by the All India Council for Vocational Education (AICVE), which comes under the umbrella of the MHRD. The AICVE is in charge of the planning and coordination of training programmes. At a state level, the tasks of the AICVE are supported by the State Councils for Vocational Education (SCVEs) (see Rao et al. 2014).

By way of contrast, the Directorate of Training (DGT) is subject to the MSDE and is responsible for training (see Männicke 2011; Rao et al. 2014). The DGT is in charge of the formulation of guidelines for the development of educational standards and technical requirements (see DGT 2014e). The National Council of Vocational Training (NCVT) provides advisory support. The members of the NCVT comprise central and state ministries, employer and employee associations and the AICTE (see Wessels 2012) (see also Chapter 5.2).

4.3 Summary of forms of provision and the training programmes aligned to them

The following sub-chapters present the vocational provision in detail.

4.3.1 Craftsmen Training Scheme

The Craftsmen Training Scheme (CTS) has been in existence since the 1950s and is lead managed by the MSDE in conjunction with the DGT. In purely numerical terms, craft trade training is the most important training programme in the formal vocational training system. Training takes place in institutions run by state and private ITIs.

India has a total of 11,964 training institutes with a capacity of around 1.7 million training places in 126 training occupations. Of these institutes, 2,284 are state ITIs and 9,680 are private ITIs (see DGT 2015d).

Of the total of 126 training occupations, 73 are technically aligned and 48 are non-technical in nature[11] (plus five training courses for visually impaired persons). Depending on the training course, duration of training varies between six months and two years. Commencement of training may take place after completion of the eighth, tenth or twelfth class contingent on the respective occupation.

---

11 Non-technical training occupations may include both craft trade occupations such as baker, tailor or gardener and commercial occupations like computer user, office assistant or marketing assistant. A precise division of technical and non-technical training occupations is available at: http://dget.nic.in/content/innerpage/trade-syllabus.php.

In accordance with national stipulations, training is split into 70 per cent practical instruction and 30 per cent theory. The theoretical element includes occupationally-related contents and units for the personal development of pupils (see GoI 2015).

The standardised curricula are set by the NCVT, and these committees are afforded organisational support by the DGT. Implementation of the curricula takes place via State Educational Committees. Curricular development is one of the core competencies of the NCVT. The NCVT also focuses on further tasks within the scope of the Skill Development Programme. These include maintenance of educational standards, stipulation of norms for conditions of admission, accreditation of institutions, development of examination procedures and certification of examinations. At state level, there are State Councils of Vocational Training (SCVTs), which assume responsibility for comparable tasks for the respective federal state. The relevant SCVTs are advised by the NCVT (see MoLE 2014, p. 243).

Many curricula for training in the craft trades have been revised in terms of content over recent years. These revised and competence-oriented curricula have been linked to the National Skills Qualifications Framework (NSQF) (see Table 34). Table 20 provides an example section from the curriculum for the training occupation of turner, which is aligned to reference level 4 of the NSQF (see also Table 34).

Table 20: NSQF level 4 [turner]

Level	Process required	Professional knowledge	Professional skill	Core skill	Responsibility
4	Work in familiar, predictable routine situation of clear choice	Factual knowledge of field of knowledge or study	Recall and demonstrate practical skill, routine and repetition in narrow range of application, using appropriate rule and tool, using quality concepts	Language to communicate written or oral, with required clarity, skill of basic arithmetic and algebraic principles, basic understanding of social political and natural environment	Responsibility for own work and learning

Source: DGT 2015b

A further component of the revised curricula is presentation of the weekly workload. Table 21 illustrates the actual ratio between theory and practice in training. In the case of the training occupation of turner, 62.5 per cent of training time is reserved for practice. This approximately corresponds to the stipulation stated above for 70 per cent practical instruction and 30 per cent theory.

Table 21: Distribution of training [turner] [hourly basis]

Total hours/ week	Trade practical	Trade theory	Workshop	Engineering drawing	Employability skills	Extra-curri-cular activity
40	25	6	2	3	2	2

Source: DGT 2015b

Despite some reforms, the CTS programme is an object of constant criticism. The quality of training features a number of deficits. Companies complain that those completing the programme are not ready for deployment on the labour market. They lack skills with regard to the practical application of what they have learned and problem solving. Further training on the job is frequently necessary in order to bring them up to speed with the practical requirements of the company (see Mehrotra et al. 2014).

However, it is not only the companies that find this kind of training very unattractive. The negative way in which it is viewed is also reflected in growing drop-out rates. Given the immense increase in training capacity, these rates are relatively high. The drop-out rate at state ITIs is 15.5 per cent, although it is significantly lower at the private ITIs, where only 6.4 per cent leave training prematurely (see Mehrotra 2014, p. 101). Two of the reasons for premature ending of training are a lack of practical relevance and the poor prospects of finding employment upon completion of the programme (see Mehrotra 2014, p. 105).

According to an IAMR study of 1,999 state ITI trainees conducted in 1999, 33 per cent still had no permanent contract of employment more than 18 months after graduating from the scheme. Of the remaining respondents surveyed, 45 per cent were in paid work, 4.5 per cent had entered self-employment, 2.1 per cent were working in a family company and 13.8 per cent were endeavouring to pursue continuing training (see Mehrotra 2014, p. 103).

In order to simplify the transition from training to working life, all state and private ITIs have so-called placement offices. The main task of these is to place those completing the programme with companies. A study (see IAMR Survey 2010) has made it clear that these activities have produced only a moderate degree of success. The average rate of successful job placement is only 16.4 per cent. Despite the professional assistance offered by the educational establishments, this indicates that effective progression into the world of work by those completing the programme at a state or private ITI is highly unlikely.

In order to compensate for the deficits of the CTS scheme, various innovation programmes have been instigated within the framework of the Vocational Training Improvement Project (VTIP). One of these initiatives, often regarded as an upgrade to the conventional CTS programme, is the Centre of Excellence (CoE) Initiative (Tara/Kumar 2017). The essential core of this programme comprises an attempt to achieve a paradigm shift away from the traditional monolithic structure of training with one point of entry and exit and to move towards a multi-skilling scheme which provides the option of flexible access and departure within the training process. It also represents a move from single-focus training at a VET institution in favour of an institutionally mixed or dual model which is characterised by theoretical training at an educational establishment and practical training in the company. The main aim is to offer those completing the programme good opportunities on the labour market by covering the companies' demand for well-trained workers.

In this model, the first year of training comprises Broad Based Basic Training (BBBT). This is followed by Advanced Modules and Specialised Modules (AM and SM) in the second year. The essential features of the CoE are listed below.

▶ BBBT consists of a total of six modules, each of which is of two months' duration. The objective is that training should provide preparation for a particular industrial sector (see example for the IT sector in Table 22).

▶ AM courses last for six months and take place in the first half of the second year of training.

▶ BBBT and AM curricula are developed via a cooperative approach with the companies involved, and standardised curricula are in place across India.

▶ Final examinations (AITT) for BBBT and AM are conducted centrally under the supervision of the NCVT.

▶ Those successfully completing the programme are awarded a National Trade Certificate (NTC) both for BBBT and for AM.

▶ Training via the SM takes place in the second half of the second year of training. Final examinations and certifications are organised and issued in conjunction with the state government and industry. The training is recognised by the central NCVT.

Table 22: BBBT modules in the field of information technology

Modules
Basic electrical and electronics
Basic assembling and maintenance of PCs
Basic computer networking
Basic office automation
Basic Internet and multimedia
Basic database processing

Source: ITI Bhavnagar 2005

A total of 1,396 state ITIs have been upgraded thus far through cooperation between private and state institutions under the Public-Private Partnership (PPP) programme (see DGT 2014a; DGT 2011).

4.3.2 Apprenticeship Training Scheme (ATS)

Dual apprentice training under the ATS was established in 1961. Dual training in India refers to training at state school-based institutions in conjunction with on-the-job training at participating companies.

A distinction is made between four different types of apprentice training. The MHRD is responsible for the first three of these, whereas the fourth comes under the auspices of the DGT.

(1) Graduate Apprenticeship (graduate level)
(2) Technician Apprenticeship (diploma level)
(3) Technician Vocational Apprenticeship (technical graduate level)
(4) Trade Apprenticeship[12]

Within this context, mention should also be made of the Informal Apprenticeship, which is not subject to any state institution and acts as its own provider (see DGT 2015e). Because this form of training is particularly relevant in India, it will be addressed separately at a later point (see Chapter 4.6).

The main goals of apprenticeship training are as follows:

▻   Facilitation of practical training for young trainees

▻   Networking of industry and technical institutions to improve the quality of technical training and develop human capital

▻   Ensuring that training takes place at various institutions (public and private)

▻   Development and implementation of training modules for trainees with the involvement of industry, the apprentices themselves and other institutions affected

▻   Imparting practical aspects of theoretical training with the assistance of various didactic media and methods

▻   Issuing of final certificates in the event of successful completion of training

▻   Improving the technical know-how of young people and strengthening the self-confidence of trainees (GoI 2013)

---

12   Optional Trade Apprenticeship: Since the amendment of the Apprentices Act in 2014, new occupational designations may be determined by employers (see summary of current changes—Apprentices (Amendment) Act 2014, see below).

Graduate Apprenticeship, Technician Apprenticeship and Technician Vocational Apprenticeship

Responsibility for the Graduate Apprenticeship, Technician Apprenticeship and Technician Vocational Apprenticeship programmes rests with the MHRD. The monitoring process is shared by Regional Boards of Apprenticeship (BoAT) in Kanpur, Mumbai and Chennai and the Board of Practical Training (BoPT) in Kolkata (see DGT 2014a, p. 268; MHRD 2016b). A total of 126 training occupations are offered within the area of Graduate and Technician Apprenticeships. In the case of the Technician Vocational Apprenticeship, two training occupations have been added to bring the number to 128. Duration of training in the three postgraduate programmes is one year. Of a total of 131,379 training places available, 71,233 were filled and successfully completed. This means that take-up is only 54 per cent (see Table 23). Certificate takes place via the Department of Education, which is subject to the MHRD (see MHRD 2014, p. 269).

Table 23: Training statistics for Graduate, Technician and Technician (Vocational) Apprentices (status: 31 December 2013)

	Graduate	Technician	Technician (Vocational)	Total
Total number of training places	54,749	48,643	27,987	131,379
Number of training places filled	30,055	33,554	7,624	71,233
Number of training places filled in %	55	69	27	54
Minorities				
Scheduled Caste (SC), number	1,318	2,734	1,005	5,057
Scheduled Caste (SC) in %	4	8	13	9
Scheduled Tribes (ST), number	210	388	291	889
Scheduled Tribes (ST) in %	1	1	4	1
Minorities/disadvantaged groups, number	1,516	1,112	328	3,398
Minorities/disadvantaged groups in %	5	3	4	4
Persons with disabilities (PwD), number	37	80	16	133
Persons with disabilities (PwD) in %	0.12	0.24	0.21	0.19
Women, number	8,244	4,866	3,671	16,781
Women in %	27	15	48	24

Source: MoLE 2014, p. 273

Courses are offered at 12,687 school-based institutions which are aligned to the guidelines of the Central Apprenticeship Council (CAC) (see Mehrotra 2014, p. 224).

Trainees receive a monthly allowance. Fifty per cent of this is paid by the central government and 50 per cent by the employers (see MHRD 2016b). The amount of the training allowance is adjusted every two years on the basis of the Consumer Prices Index (see Mehrotra 2014, p. 135). Table 24 below lists the monthly training allowances (as of 19 December 2014) for the respective training programmes (see MHRD 2016b).[13]

Table 24: Allowance paid for the various training programmes [in euro/per month]

	Year	Graduate	Technician	Technician (Voc.)
Earning [in euro]	2010*	Approx. 48	Approx. 38	Approx. 26.50
Earning [in euro]	2014**	Approx. 67	Approx. 48	Approx. 37

Source: * Mehrotra 2014, p. 135; ** MHRD 2016b

Summary of current changes

Apprentice training has been an integral component of vocational education and training in India since 1961 and was most recently adapted in 2014. Prior to this, various amendments had already been made to update the programme and adjust it to meet requirements (see Mehrotra 2014, p. 135). The name of the programme was formally changed in the Apprentices (Amendment) Act 2014. The most important recent alterations are summarised below.

▶ **Designation** – two further definitions have been added to the previous names of training occupations (optional trade and portal site), meaning that employers can also opt for new occupational titles with immediate effect.

▶ **Minimum age** – the minimum age in certain dangerous industrial occupations has been raised from 14 to 18.

▶ **Number of trainees** – the central government acts in conjunction with the CAC to stipulate the number of trainees for the respective areas of training.

▶ **Cooperation with employers** – several employers can join forces to offer practical training together.

▶ **Practical training for trainees** – each company providing training must prepare the workplace in such a way so as to enable practical training to take place in an appropriate form. This was previously ensured via an approval procedure, but checks are no longer conducted.

▶ **Basic education for trainees** – basic education may take place at any institution which is adequately equipped.

---

13   The cost of living in India is lower than in Germany.

- ▶ **Awarding of certificates** – the amended legislation states that any authorised authority may issue a certificate.

- ▶ **Hours of work, overtime, leave and public holidays** – weekly and daily working hours are governed by law. The amended legislation states that working times and leave may be determined at the discretion of the employer or in accordance with company policy.

- ▶ **Penalties and measures** – the law states that particular offences relating to non-compliance with stipulations may be punishable by six months' imprisonment or by an unspecified fine. A current draft law sets out that the maximum level of the fine must be determined in advance and that imprisonment as a punishment should be removed (see PRS 2016).

Trade Apprenticeship

The prerequisite for entry to a Trade Apprenticeship is a school certificate from the eighth, tenth or twelfth class and a minimum age of 14. Duration of training varies between six months and four years depending on the training occupation (see Table 25).

Table 25: Training occupations and respective duration of training (examples on the basis of selected training occupations)

Training occupation	Duration
Weaver	6 months
Hairdresser	
Glass former	1 year
Gardener	
Tailor	1½ years
Secretarial assistant	
Car mechanic	2 years
Producer of leather goods	
Railway worker	3 years
Welder	
Turner	
Draughtsman/woman	
Mould- and toolmaker	4 years
Tools mechanic	

Source: MHRD 2014, pp. 278 ff.

Dual training of apprentices is taking place at approximately 28,500 participating companies in various specific specialist industrial groups. Under the Apprenticeship Act, a contract is concluded between the company providing training and the apprentice.

Another aspect comparable to the German system is that apprentices in India receive a training allowance. This allowance is, however, far below the level of earnings available to German trainees. An Indian apprentice usually earns between 28 and 42 euro per month (DGT 2014a, p. 269), whereas a German trainee can expect to receive between 400 and 1,400 euro per month (depending on training occupation and year of training)[14] (see BIBB 2015). In making this comparison, however, account needs to be taken of living costs, average monthly income and the Purchase Price Index.

Table 26: Training statistics for the Trade Apprenticeship programme

	Central sector	Public/private sector	Total
Total number of training places	53,028	306,328	359,356
Number of training places filled	339,45	177,687	211,632
Number of training places filled in %	64	58	59
Minorities/disadvantaged groups			
Scheduled Caste (SC), number	5,761	20,617	26,378
Scheduled Caste (SC) in %	12	12	12
Scheduled Tribes (ST), number	1,462	9,345	10,807
Scheduled Tribes (ST) in %	4	5	5
Minorities, number	1,164	7,152	8,316
Minorities in %	3	4	4
Persons with disabilities (PwD), number	255	546	801
Persons with disabilities (PwD) in %	1	0.3	0.3
Women, number	1,417	7,854	9,271
Women in %	4	4	4

Source: MoLE 2014

Basic theoretical training for the Trade Apprenticeship is delivered at state centres which are also referred to as Basic Training Centres (BTC) or Related Instruction Centres (RIC). The practical part of training takes place in the participating companies. Of a total of

---

14   For example, an electronics technician receives €929 in the first year of training, €980 in the second year of training, €1,051 in the third year of training and €1,108 in the fourth year of training. A hairdresser earns €394 in the first year of training, €493 in the second year of training, and €596 in the third year of training.

360,000 training places available under the Trade Apprenticeship scheme, only 212,000 have been filled thus far (see Table 26). This means that take-up is only 59 per cent (see Mehrotra 2014; GoI 2015). The reasons for this low take-up or participation rate are the low training allowance and the absence of any guarantee of a job following successful completion of training (Mehrotra 2014).

Apprentices have a wide choice of 259 training occupations in a total of 39 specialist areas (see Mehrotra 2014; GoI 2015). As already mentioned, the DGT is responsible for this form of training at a central level and monitoring is spread across six regional directorates located in Kolkata, Mumbai, Chennai, Hyderabad, Kanour und Faridabad (see DGT 2014a, p. 268). The NCVT conducts final examinations in AITT form twice a year. Those successfully completing the programme are awarded the National Apprenticeship Certificate (NAC) (see Mehrotra 2014; GoI 2015).

Summary

A study conducted by the World Bank and the International Labour Organization (ILO) (2013) summarised the following weak points within the Apprenticeship Training scheme:

▶ Very low level of participation in the training system by employers and employees

▶ Very low level of training allowance

▶ High regulatory requirements for employers, high penalties in the case of non-compliance

▶ Shortage of well-trained teachers and trainers

▶ Poor infrastructure at the training institutes (state ITIs) (see also Chapter 4.3.1)

▶ Low level of provision of training courses in the services sector, where there is high employment potential

▶ Low level of provision of apprenticeships in rural regions

▶ Parts of the curriculum are obsolete and inflexible

▶ Lack of cooperation between the various educational institutions

▶ Low rates of employment after completion of training

▶ Lack of vertical mobility to enable trainees to achieve higher qualification levels

▶ Lack of commitment on the part of employers or industry to the development and revision of curricula

4.3.3 Bachelor of Vocation (B. Voc.)

The Bachelor of Vocation (B. Voc.) programme was introduced by the UGC in 2014 as part of the Skill Development Initiative. This is a scheme which facilitates vertical and horizontal mobility. The minimum entry requirement is completion of class 12. Programmes comprise 40 per cent general educational content and 60 per cent vocational education and training content. The particular features of this scheme are the involvement of industrial partners and an option to finish the programme after one, two or three years and still receive a qualification. Re-entry is also possible (see Table 27). Programmes are offered at universities and colleges alongside other "undergraduate programmes" (see UGC 2014). Over the next five years (status 2015), 25 per cent of institutions of higher education must offer special career-oriented courses. These courses must also be embedded in the NSQF. The plan is for account to be taken of the relevant qualifications when this categorisation is undertaken (MSDE 2015).

Table 27: Bachelor of Vocation qualifications

Qualification	Duration [in years]	NSQF level
Diploma	1	5
Advanced Diploma	2	6
B. Voc. Degree	3	7

Source: UGC 2014

The general education curriculum is aligned to the normal standards of the respective university or college, and there is a further plan to integrate language and communication courses. The vocational components of the curriculum are oriented to the requirements of industry with the aim of making those completing the programme ready for deployment on the labour market. On-the-job training elements and project work are included for this purpose. The introduction of the B. Voc. was also accompanied by stipulations relating to credits and suggested time allocations which are at the same time contained within the NSQF (see Table 28). One credit corresponds to 15 learning units of 60 minutes each. This applies equally to theory, practice and units comprising exercises. Credits are to be applied usefully. The intention is that completion of a practical placement or of self-directed learning using qualified information made available within an electronic system (e-content) should take up about half as much time as participation in lectures and workshops (UGC 2014).

Table 28: Stipulation of credits for B. Voc.

NSQF level	Credits for vocational and practical education	Credits for general education	Duration	Qualification
3rd year	36	24	6 semesters	B. Voc.
2nd year	36	24	4 semesters	Advanced Diploma
1st year	36	24	2 semesters	Diploma
Total	108	72		

Source: UGC 2015

Final examinations for the general theoretical element take place in accordance with the standards of the respective institution. Examination of the practical vocational components is conducted by the relevant SSCs.

4.4 In-company training

One serious problem for pupils in formal vocational training, in particular at the state and private ITIs, is the lack of any harmonisation with representatives of trade and industry and the absence of any revision of the curricula. This means that the necessary practical relevance is only included in teaching at the margins (see Mehrotra et al. 2014). The estimation is that 58 per cent of young people are barely in possession of appropriate practically relevant skills. In the formal sector, this represents a greater problem than unemployment (see Ramasamy/Mani 2016, p. 171). In order to compensate for the deficits of applicants, subsequent training needs to be given and an extensive induction process needs to be provided in the company (training on the job) in cases where more demanding positions are to be filled (Zenner/Pilz 2015).

According to the Planning Commission (2008), 80 per cent of career entrants have no chance of receiving such internal company training measures (see Ramasamy/Mani 2016, p. 171).

In a study on the Indian qualification strategy, Mehrotra (2014) therefore calls for training measures in two areas in particular. In his view, there needs to be rapid employment of job seekers, and persons changing jobs must be provided with continuing training.

Some major Indian companies such as Tata, Accenture, Infosys and Maruti are able to display important initiatives in this regard (Ramasamy/Mani 2016), and indeed German companies including VW, Bosch and Festo are offering excellent vocational training courses in India (see Chapter 5.7.1). Tata Consultancy Service (TCS) will provide an example of how company-based training and internal company programmes can be successfully delivered.

TCS India is a multinational and one of the ten most successful IT companies in the world. It has 150 locations/branches in 46 countries and employs more than 300,000 staff in the IT/ITES sector. New employees undertake an Initial Learning Programme (ILP), which includes modules in various disciplines such as basic technical training, project development, life cycle management and soft skills. Each staff member also completes a mandatory 14-day continuing training programme each year in order to foster ongoing or lifelong learning. Beside this provision, there are also various online courses of which employees are informed via email or text. TCS gives special support to talented workers identified by line managers. These high-performing individuals complete further technical and management training courses. Measures aimed at ensuring that employees are deployed in a versatile way also include participation in various projects or placements abroad (Badrinath 2016).

4.5 Vocational provision of non-governmental organisations (NGOs)

Not-for-profit bodies such as foundations, church institutions, academic think tanks and other organisations are all active in India. Although NGOs are registered with the central government, they are managed in accordance with the country's rules, regulations and laws by the members themselves and by associated persons. No controls are undertaken by central government (NGO India year of publication not stated). NGOs address topics such as human rights, gender differences and discrimination, healthcare, agricultural development, social matters, the environment, and indigenous and disadvantaged groups. Logically, NGOs are therefore also actively involved in the educational sector in many regards (see Gengaiah 2016).

The NGOs active in India can be divided up into trusts, societies and non-profit companies. The respective provisions and registration requirements are set out in the relevant laws (NGO India year of publication not stated).

NGOs receive grants from various sources. These include member contributions, private and public donations, grants given by local, national and foreign funding organisations and foundations, financing via the government, sale of products and services, and CSR funds of private sector companies (see Chapter 5.3.1). These funds are needed to finance measures, salaries and other general costs.[15] One example of a national not-for-profit development organisation will be presented below.

The Action for Welfare and Awakening in Rural Environment (AWARE) programme was launched in Hyderabad in the federal state of Andhra Pradesh (today Telangana) in 1975. Its aim is to help people to help themselves by providing support in areas such as rights and responsibilities, protection of human rights and encouragement of gender equality. Alongside these intentions, the programme includes a broad range of vocational

---

15 The in-company training and vocational provision offered by NGOs plays only a marginal role compared to the informal sector.

training schemes on topics including management responsibility, competence development, agriculture, animal husbandry, health promotion and environmental education. AWARE is a target-group specific, adapted and temporary programme which assists and supports village inhabitants along the pathway to self-realisation. AWARE has helped a total of 8,760 village communities and approximately 2.5 million people in the federal states of Andhra Pradesh, Orissa, Maharashtra, Gujarat, Uttar Pradesh, Uttaranchal, Kerala, Karnataka and Tamil Nadu (AWARE 2017).

4.6 Informal vocational education and training

Whereas in Europe the term "informal learning" is used to describe any kind of learning "resulting from daily activities related to work, family or leisure [...] not organised or structured in terms of objectives, time or learning support [and] mostly unintentional from the learner's perspective" (Cedefop 2009, p. 86), a different understanding applies within the Indian context. A number of central aspects need to be explained in order to comprehend this divergent view.

The traditional system of informal education in India is referred to as the Gurukul System (see Chapter 3.1). This is an old educational concept via which knowledge is imparted and passed on within a family. The teacher (guru) acts as a leader, father and role model. In its time, the Gurukul System offered instruction in weaponry, music, art, self-defence and religious teachings. This part of the training was, however, reserved for the elite. Occupational competencies were passed on from generation to generation. Because of societal acceptance, there was no documentary certification of this process (see Singh 2013, p. 107).

In today's India, the educational activities that are described as "informal" are all those which do not form part of the state-recognised general educational system (see Chapter 3.4) or which are not aligned to the conventional state-run VET system (see Chapter 4.3). This makes the difference to the European understanding clear. In India, VET activities may be designated as "informal" even if they are financed and certified by the state. This means that such provision comprises "special programmes" or activities which are initiated by the central state or individual federal states as an addition to the traditional structures in order to cover certain needs or meet specific objectives. It is precisely this multitude of different sorts of provision, which in some cases exist for only short periods of time, that leads to confusing complexity. This has also been an object of criticism. Educational policy has been accused in part of pursuing a strong course of actionism instead of a clear strategy and of putting regional and vested interests to the fore (Prasad 2016).

Beside the large informal sector, the Indian understanding also of course includes informal learning as viewed in Europe. The consequence of all of this is that the Indian version of informal learning is defined in much broader terms than in other countries.

The present publication takes this wide-ranging understanding on board in order to ensure consistency of the statements made here with those contained in other literature sources relating to Indian vocational education and training.

The greatest challenge that India needs to face is the recognition, validation and accreditation of both formal learning and, against the background of the immense significance of the informal sector, of informal learning too (see Chapter 5.6.2). Within the scope of the debate on competence, several programmes for this purpose have been instigated over recent years (see Chapter 5.8), some of which take the form of public-private partnerships. The most important "informal vocational educational activities" from an Indian point of view are briefly presented below.

Informal vocational teaching follows the "watch and learn" principle. This is a simple training concept which involves the apprentice in the work processes in the company. The trainee thus learns both via participation and via instruction provided by a trainer within the company (see Mehrotra 2014; Sodhi/Wessels 2016; Pilz et al. 2015a).

A total of 35 Community Polytechnics were established by the central government in 1978. This sort of informal training involves short-term measures delivered in modular courses with a duration of between three and six months, depending on regional requirements and the infrastructure available at a local level. The programme is directed at unemployed young people, school and college drop-outs, and other disadvantaged groups such as the underprivileged rural population (SC, ST and OBC). Young people are able to undergo training in various programmes and have the opportunity to acquire a range of competencies. In 2013, there was a total of 617 AICTE-inspected institutions (Mehrotra 2014, p. 56).

Other important state programmes are Jan Shikshan Sansthan (JSS), Shramik Vidyapeeths, and the Khadi and Village Industries Commission (KVIC). These programmes are aimed at adults who are unable to read and write or who left school prematurely. They are also frequently offered in rural areas in order to strengthen the local population and their economic situation. Krishi Vigyan Kendras (KVK), for example, is directed at workers in the primary sector and at young people in country regions in particular. This measure attempts to close the gap between available technologies and the application of such technologies in order to increase productivity. They frequently take the form of on-farm training sessions which take an instruction-based approach to present areas of potential for increasing production. This sort of training is practical and participant-oriented and aims to strengthen awareness of changes amongst farmers (see Sodhi/Wessels 2016).

In overall terms, therefore, we may conclude that the predominant goals of this provision are the strengthening of individual practical skills and the facilitation of labour market access within a short space of time. The main focus is on rural regions, on disadvantaged groups and on promoting self-employment or regular work following completion of a training programme (see Ramasamy 2016; Wessels/Pilz 2016).

Measurement of competencies in many of these programmes takes place with the assistance of the National Vocational Qualifications Framework (NVQF). As presented in Chapter 3.3, the NVEQF places its emphasis on comparability of general and vocational qualifications whereas the NVQF, on the other hand, concentrates on the recognition of skills in the organised and non-organised sector. In accordance with the Indian interpretation, informal training activities and learning in the workplace in particular are included. The NVQF facilitates vertical mobility from vocational to academic learning. It also fosters lifelong learning via improved recognition of qualifications and of skills and learning outcomes previously acquired via formal or informal means. Chapter 5.6.2 addresses the amalgamation of the two national qualifications frameworks to create the NSQF (see Singh 2013, p. 110).

However, alongside these forms of learning which are at least partially organised or subsequently formalised, genuinely informal training activities continue to play a significant role in Indian society. In the craft trades and in agriculture in particular, the passing on of specialist knowledge and of abilities and skills to the next generation forms a central part of family life. In many cases, this leads to a highly fruitful combination of acquisition of profession with acquisition of income (see Jung/Pilz 2016; Pilz/Wilmshöfer 2015c; Pilz et al. 2015a).

4.7 Specific programmes for women

Although India is a secular and democratic state, women have a lesser social status than men in some cases. The rights of women are frequently pre-defined by their family or husband, a situation which is particularly discernible in rural regions (see bpb 2007). For this reason, modern Indian educational policy attaches a particular significance to the training, employment and continuing training of women.

Vocational courses for females are offered in the form of "Women Training" schemes. These are regular VET courses realised as part of the craft trade (CTS) and instructor training (CITS) programmes (see also Chapter 5.4). In India, there is a total of eleven institutions which have specialised in the training of women. There is one national institution, the National Vocational Training Institute (NVTI) in Noida, and ten regional training centres, the Regional Vocational Training Institutes (RVTI). The programme is financed by central government. There are 1,988 places available for craft trade training (CTS) and 4,080 for instructor training (CITS). Short-term programmes are also offered alongside regular training in cases where the facilities at the training centres permit this (see DGT 2015c).

At the central training centre in Noida, six training occupations are covered within the scope of the CTS and CITS programmes, respectively (see Table 29 and Table 30).

As well as the state ITIs and private ITIs, institutions especially for women also exist: the Women Industrial Training Institutes (WITIs). There is a total of 1,454 institutions with 78,080 available places spread across independent WITIs and female-specific courses at state ITIs (status 2012). The courses are Basic Skill Courses delivered in accordance with the CTS training plan in a total of 67 technical and 60 non-technical training occupations approved by the NCVT. In addition to the special institutions for women, there is a quota reserved for females at the state ITIs. This accounts for around 25–30 per cent of places and thus makes up a comparatively small proportion of training volume in the craft trades (see DGT 2014a, p. 284).

Table 29: Training occupations in the CTS programme for women

Training occupation	Further information
Computer operator and programming assistant (COPA)	Available places
Desktop publishing user	▶ COPA – 40 places per cohort
Secretarial assistant	▶ Other subjects – 16 places
Hair and skin care	▶ Duration – 1 or 2 years
Technical draftswoman	(Module of a duration of 6 months)
Electronics mechanic	Access requirement – completion of class 10

Source: DGT 2015c

Table 30: Training occupations in the CITS programme for women

Training occupation	Further information
Dressmaking	Available places
Embroidery	▶ 20 places per module
Secretarial assistant	Duration – each training occupation comprises four modules (of three months each)
Hair and skin care	Access requirement –
Technical draftswoman	▶ National Trade Certificate via NCVT
Electronics mechanic	▶ Diploma in a comparable subject via AICTE

Source: DGT 2015b

5 Important general conditions and factors determining vocational education and training

This chapter will begin by presenting a number of important laws within the context of Indian education or vocational education and training. Further references to these general legal conditions are provided at some points within the text.

Other significant general conditions for VET will then be depicted.

5.1 Legal standardisation of vocational education and training and school-based and company-based training

Initial regulatory processes which still exert an influence on the educational system today were stipulated under British rule. Important general conditions were put in place following independence in 1947.

One major milestone was the introduction of training in the craft trades via the 1961 Apprenticeship Act. This is a nationwide law which establishes the provisions for trainees (access qualification, training contract, reserved quotas for castes) and for the structuring of the training itself (duration, contents) (see Chapter 4.3.2).

Two further reforms were instigated prior to the turn of the millennium. From 1964 to 1966, the Kothari Commission investigated the Indian education system with the aim of creating standardised general principles and guidelines for the development of education. Its work proved pivotal to the further development of vocational education and training and in 1968 led to one of the most important educational reforms in India's history: the introduction of a uniform educational structure under the joint responsibility of central government and the federal states. During the further course of the process, curricular structures were developed and later standardised (see Chapter 5.7.3). As a result of the universalisation of elementary education and associated measures to secure the infrastructure, the central government assumed control over the development of the public school system in the federal states.

In 2002, the introduction of the Sarva Shiksha Abhiyan (SSA)—known in English as "Education for All"—laid the foundations for an upgrading of vocational education and training. This programme endeavours to improve human capabilities from early childhood in order to open up an opportunity for high-quality education in the future. National programmes aimed at strengthening VET such as the National Policy on Skill Development (NPSD) and the introduction of the National Vocational Education Qualification Framework (NVEQF) will be presented in more detail later in the handbook.

5.2 Governance structures in vocational education and training and school-based and company-based training

In order to localise governance structures in Indian vocational education and training in clear terms, the competent bodies can be divided into central and state institutions. The MHRD and the MSDE are the most important central institutions and are responsible for the financing and administration of VET programmes. At a national level, the AICTE and the DGT are subordinate to the MHRD and the MSDE, respectively. The AICTE and the DGT are responsible for the formulation of standards, the stipulation of norms, the distribution of financial grants to educational establishments, the monitoring of educational programmes, examinations and certification procedures, and further VET matters within the sub-systems aligned to their ministries (see Majumdar 2008, pp. 25 ff.). Day-to-day administrative affairs are incumbent on the respective federal state governments and union territory administrations.

Advisory functions are performed by two tripartite committees (comprising members from central and state government and the union territories and representatives of the employers and trade unions). These are the National Council of Vocational Training (NCVT) and the Central Apprenticeship Council (CAC). Both these bodies are responsible for the determination of training guidelines, for training standards and for the examination and certification of training programmes. The NCVT and CAC also issue recommendations for the introduction of new training occupations or for the updating of training occupations which have become obsolete. At federal state level, the State Councils of Vocational Training (SCVT) are responsible for the above tasks.

Other ministries and state government bodies are also responsible for the implementation of VET programmes besides the MSDE and the MHRD. The centralised and federal structure of the sub-continent exerts a strong influence on educational policy and administration (see Lang-Wojtasik 2013). This structure results in an absence of co-operation between the ministries responsible and also leads to dissonances between the individual states. In the area of vocational education and training, the aim is to reduce this lack of cooperation between ministries in particular via the establishment of the new Ministry of Skill Development (see 5.8.1), which will bundle areas of responsibility for educational programmes within a single ministry.

There are also regional imbalances between the states. A study carried out by the NSDC (2012) (see Chapter 5.8.2) made it clear that blue-collar jobs predominate in the states of Bihar, Rajasthan, Uttar Pradesh, Chattisgarh and Andhra Pradesh. This means that expansion of or support for ITIs could have a much greater effect here than in other federal states (see Pillay 2014).

As already described at the outset (see Chapter 4.2), the formal part of vocational education and training in India can be sub-divided into vocational education, vocational training, tertiary vocational education, and continuing vocational education and training.

Most of the education and training providers are upper secondary schools, ITIs, polytechnics, JSS, NIOS and further VET providers. The most important areas of responsibility for the CTS and ATS programmes are summarised in Table 31.

Table 31: Areas of responsibility of the CTS and ATS

Training scheme	Provider	Govt. of India	State Govt.	Industry
Craftsmen Training Scheme (CTS)	State and private Industrial Training Institutes (ITIs)	Responsible for policy and procedure, standards, duration etc. in consultation with the NCVT Conduct final trade tests on behalf of NCVT Responsibility with the MSDE	Administration of the institutes	Advise central and state governments at national and institutional level Assist in the final trade tests
Apprenticeship Training Scheme (ATS)	Graduate Apprenticeship (graduate level) Technician Apprenticeship (diploma level) Technician Vocational Apprenticeship (technical graduate level) Trade Apprenticeship	Responsible for policy, procedure, notification of industries, designation of trades, syllabi, standards etc. in consultation with the CAC Assist with coordination of the programmes Concurrent jurisdiction with the states to assist, coordinate and regulate programmes in private sector industries Conduct final trade tests on behalf of NCVT Responsibility with the MSDE	Assist with, coordinate and regulate programmes in central public sector industries Impart related instructions Impart basic training in the case of those industries in the private sector which employ fewer than 500 workers	Implementation of the practical training programme in accordance with the Apprenticeship Act (Training Law) Arrange for basic training (by employers, employing more than 500 workers) Advise the central and state governments at national and state level

Source: DGT 2014f

There is a multitude of further education and training which is offered by a total of 19 ministries at national and state level. Some of these have been described in the preceding chapters.

5.3 Financing of vocational education and training and training

5.3.1 Financing of training

Data on the public financing of vocational education and training is virtually non-existent in India. At state level, expenditure on vocational education is documented together with spending on the general secondary sector. Expenditure on vocational training is usually summarised under individual state courses and programmes (e.g. ITI courses, ATS etc.). This makes the disaggregation of financing outgoings extremely difficult (see World Bank 2008, p. 96). Vocational education and training programmes are financed by the central and state governments (see Gupta et al. 2016, p. 48; World Bank 2008). This form of financing is, however, limited and restrictive and cannot take full account of the enormous challenges which exist at a quantitative and qualitative level (see Pilz et al. 2015b; Tara et al. 2016). Nevertheless, the current Indian VET system is heavily dependent on public funding.

100 per cent financing on the part of the central government only takes place in respect of the following components:

▷ Apprentice training
▷ Workshops for textbook development
▷ Subsidising of teaching materials
▷ Financing of apprentice workshops and buildings
▷ Equipment for schools
▷ Teacher training
▷ Workshops for curriculum development

50 per cent state financing takes place for the following components:

▷ Vocational branch of the State Directorates of Education
▷ SCERT
▷ Vocational branch for districts
▷ Provision of materials and contingency funds for pupil excursions

In addition to this, 75 per cent and 25 per cent of the costs of vocational school teachers are funded by the central and state governments, respectively. The state governments are responsible for the full financing of examination regulations and vocational guidance services (Gupta et al. 2016).

Although private companies also finance vocational education and training programmes, these often constitute internal company training schemes or benefits in kind (see Pillay 2014) (see Chapter 4.4).

As already summarised in the preceding chapters, there are many changes regarding the financing of VET programmes. Participation by companies within the scope of PPPs is a particular initiative via which the costs arising are distributed across various stakeholders (DGT 2014a).

5.3.2 Corporate social responsibility (CSR)

The 2013 Companies Act transformed the notion of corporate social responsibility (CSR) into a statutory stipulation. The law states that companies must make a social contribution to society to the value of at least two per cent of average net profits over the past three years (from 2013). This requirement is incumbent on all companies registered via the Companies Act (comparable to the Trade Registry in Germany). It applies to both domestic firms and the subsidiaries of foreign companies. The law does, however, provide for differentiation. Companies with an annual turnover of €76 million or more, companies with equity in the amount of €134 and above and companies with a net profit of €0.67 million or above are all required to make a CSR contribution (see CII/PwC 2013). According to the Economic Times, India's top 75 companies paid more than €5.35 million to CSR in 2015. These include the company group Reliance, Infosys and TCS, which made contributions of approx. €1 million, €0.32 million and around €0.3 million, respectively. A survey conducted by KPMG (2015) reveals that revenues from the CSR fund are primarily spent in the areas of healthcare, education and the environment. In specific terms, this represents €180 million of spending on healthcare, €167 million for education and €75 million for the environment (see Figure 1).

Figure 1: CSR spending by sectors (in millions of euro)

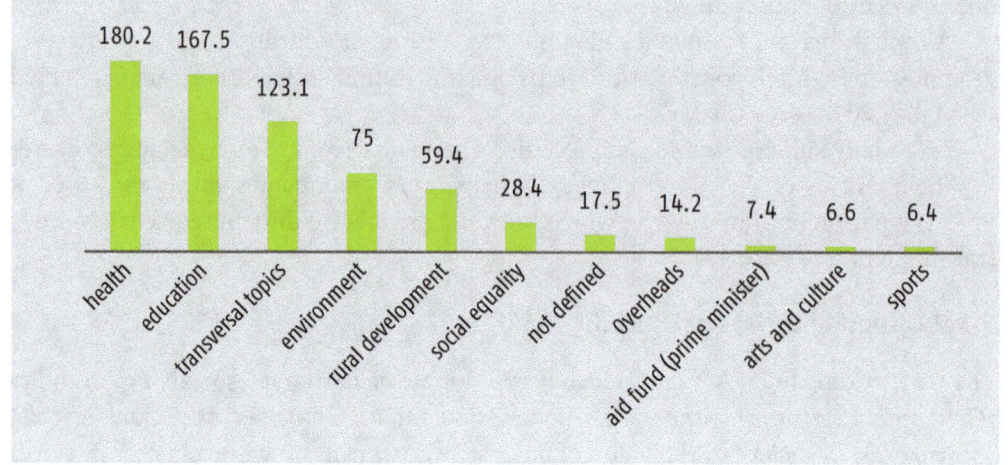

Source: Own representation, based on KMPG 2015, p. 22

5.4 Training for VET staff

As already summarised in Chapter 4 , training for VET staff can be divided into two areas. These are teacher training for the field of vocational education, which particularly encompasses the pre-vocational training programmes at secondary and upper secondary level. And secondly, there is teacher training for the area of vocational training, i.e. for VET programmes such as CTS and ATS and for training delivered at polytechnics or engineering colleges.

Teaching staff in general education or in pre-vocational education within the secondary sector (classes 9 and 10) must be in possession of a Bachelor of Education (B.Ed.) or Bachelor of Teaching (B.T.) in order to be allowed to perform their function. A further requirement is the completion of a one-year full-time higher education study programme in combination with another qualification in the form of a Bachelor degree in the specialisms of arts, science or commerce. The minimum requirement for teachers at upper secondary level (classes 11 and 12) is a Master's qualification in the relevant subject.

Teaching staff at colleges need to hold a Master's degree (Master of Education, M.Ed.) or a doctorate (PhD) (see Table 32).

Instructors at technical and vocational teaching establishments usually need to have attended a Central Training Institute (CTI) and obtained an Instructor Training Certificate (see Table 32) (see Norric 2006, p. 39).

Table 32: Levels of competence for teachers in the area of vocational education and training/pre-vocational education

Education and training area	Classes to be taught	Qualification	Access requirement	institutions
Secondary sector	Classes 9 and 10	B.Ed.	Bachelor	Postgraduate courses at university
Upper secondary level	Classes 11 and 12		Master's	
Secondary and upper secondary sector	Classes 9 to 12	BA, B.Ed. or BS B.Ed. or BCom. B.Ed.	Higher Secondary School Certificate	Colleges
Tertiary sector	College	N/A	M.Ed. or PhD	University

Source: Norric 2006, p. 39 and CBSE 2015, pp. 52 ff.

The various training programmes for teachers are summarised in Table 33. The institutions responsible for the programmes are presented in sub-chapters 5.4.1 to 5.4.4. The Central Staff Training and Research Institute (CSTARI), which also offers training programmes for instructors, is depicted in detail in Chapter 5.7.3.

Table 33: Training programmes for teaching staff in the area of vocational training

Training programme	Target group	Duration	Central government	State government	Industry
Craft Instructors Training Scheme (CITS)	Trainers at ITIs	1 year	Responsible for policy and procedure, standards and duration of programmes in consultation with the NCVT

Implementation and administration of the CTI/ATI programmes

Conduct final tests on behalf of NCVT | Delegation of ITI instructors for training at CTIs/ATIs | Advise the central government at national and institutional level

Assist with final examination |
Advanced Vocational Training Scheme (AVTS)	Industrial workers/technicians	Short-term programmes			
Supervisory training	Line managers from industry	Long-term and short-term programmes			
Women Training	Women (school leavers, trainers and others)	Long-term and short-term programmes		Delegation of female teaching staff in NVTI/RVTI	

Source: DGT 2014f; Planning Commission 2014, NCVT year of publication not stated

5.4.1 Training institutes for teaching staff

Teachers and instructors undergo training at various DGT training centres via the Craft Instructor Training Scheme (CITS). In overall terms, India has one National Craftsmen Training Institute (CTI), five regional Advanced Training Institutes (ATIs), one National Vocational Training Institute (NVTI) and twelve Regional Vocational Training Institutes (RVTIs). Teacher training covers 27 of a total of 121 specialisms (DGT 2014c). Total capacity of the institutions is around 1,600 teachers per year. This figure includes Women Training at the NVTI and RVTIs, which themselves train about 500 participants annually (see NSDC year of publication not stated, p. 83).

60,000 instructors are currently employed to teach on the CTS programme (see Chapter 4.3.1) (pupil-teacher ratio 20:1). The immense growth taking place means that the private ITIs in particular will need around 5,000 new teaching staff every year (see DGT 2014b).

The ATS programme (see Chapter 4.3.2) employs a total of 15,000 instructors. A positive growth trend is also discernible here with regard to the number of participants. For this reason, the DGT calculates that an additional 2,000 teaching staff will be required per year. Alongside this, approximately 3,000 extra instructors will be needed on an annual basis in or to counter natural processes such as leaving or retirement (see ibid.).

In overall terms for the ATS and CTS training programmes, this means that an additional volume of 10,000 instructors per year will have to be recruited (see ibid.).

5.4.2 Central Training Institute for Instructors

The Central Training Institute for Instructors opened in 1962 under the auspices of the NCVT, the DGT, the MoLE and the Government of India with support from the ILO. Training is directed at instructors at state and private ITIs. The Central Training Institute is the only national body of its kind and is located in Chennai with very good air, rail and road links. Its one-year programme is divided into four modules in the subjects of Trade Technology I (TT-I) and II (TT-II), Engineering Technology (ET) and Training Methodology (TM). Each module has a duration of three months. Prospective instructors need to pass the TT-I module before completing the TT-II module.

In these two modules, they may choose between technical (engineering) and non-technical (non-engineering) programmes. In the engineering area, there are six groups of subjects with a total of 14 specialisations in each group (DGT 2014d):

▷ Group I: Foundryman, welder, plumber, carpenter

▷ Group II: Motor vehicle mechanic, diesel mechanic

▷ Group III: Draftsman

▷ Group IV: Fitter, turner, machinist, tool & die maker

▷ Group V: Electrician

▷ Group VI: Electronics mechanic

In the non-engineering area, there are two subject groups:

- Group A: Cutting and sewing
- Group B: Computer operator and programming assistant

The access requirement for Instructor Training is possession of the National Trade Certificate (NTC) or the National Apprenticeship Certificate (NAC) (see ibid.).

Costs of training are based on form of registration. Costs of a module for civil servants delegated to the programme are the equivalent of €1.50. Costs for regular participants and participants from the SC/ST castes are €8 and €2.50, respectively. Because training is tied to a particular location, the prospective instructors are also provided with accommodation. Cost of accommodation is €4 per module (ibid.).

In order to conclude the programme successfully, candidates need to complete the four modules and pass the prescribed final examination. The modules and final examination must be fully completed within a period of three years in order to obtain the National Craft Instructor Certificate (see DGT 2014f; Ajithkumar 2016).

5.4.3 Advanced Training Institutes (ATI)

The ATIs were established by the DGT with support from the United Nations Development Programme (UNDP) and the ILO. There are seven ATIs in total, and these are located in Chennai, Hyderabad, Mumbai, Kanpur, Kolkata, Dehradrun and Ludhiana. As at the Central Training Institute for Instructors, programmes are aimed at prospective instructors at state and private ITIs or other training institutions. Courses usually last for a year and impart the "Principle of Teaching (PoT)". There are refresher courses for instructors who wish to expand their knowledge and skills or integrate the latest technologies into their teaching (see NSDC year of publication not stated, p. 82). This flagship programme is able to train up to 1,200 instructors per year (ibid.).

5.4.4 Apex Hi-Tech Institute (AHI)

The AHI is one of the projects established by the World Bank within the scope of the Vocational Training Project. It is located in Bangalore and was founded in 1993. The AHI is subject to the DGT and is financed by the central government (see DGT 2014h; Ajithkumar 2016). Training programmes are aimed at prospective ITI instructors and trainers at industrial companies and are aligned to the requirements of industry. Short-term training courses of a duration of two or three weeks are offered in the form of conventional programmes in areas such as CNS maintenance, soft skills and web design as well as in up-and-coming sectors including green technology, mobile communications and 3D solid modelling (see APEX Hi-Tech Institute year of publication not stated).

5.5 Vocational education and training research

Indian vocational education and training research is characterised by both domestic and international elements. Over recent years, international research has discussed and presented a significantly larger number of results. Indian research into the topic of "VET and continuing training" has only just begun to gain in importance. Within this process, there is a discernible trend away from the generation of pure policy papers and towards a conceptual or development-oriented approach that also encompasses empirical research (a current overview is provided by Pilz 2016a). Reference should be made in particular to highly readable studies produced by Mehrotra et al. (2015) and Pilz (2016c).

In the past, the major supernational organisations were especially responsible for ensuring research findings that displayed the requisite robustness. In 2003, for example, the ILO published an effectiveness study on state ITIs which criticised the labour market readiness of those completing programmes. A discussion paper produced by the World Bank (2008) facilitates an insight into the problems surrounding the topic of vocational education and training (state, private, informal).

Within the field of Indian research, there are various studies on the state ITIs as regards their equipment (FICCI 2006; Joshi et al. 2014) and the shortage of well-trained instructors (Joshi et al. 2014; NSDC year of publication not stated). Since the establishment of the NSDC (see Chapter 5.8.2) and the emergence of the MSDE (Chapter 5.8.1), the Indian government has been commissioning studies to look at the status quo of vocational education and training. A good summary of current changes and opportunities for improvement is, for example provided in the "National Policy for Skill Development and Entrepreneurship 2015" published by the MSDE and by a report produced by the NSDC entitled "Building Trainers' Skills in Vocational Employability".

Activity from independent VET research is very small compared to these state-organised approaches. Universities have, for example, been very slow to recognise the relevance of this research thrust. One of the causes of this situation is likely to be the fact that university-based vocational school teacher training complete with integrated research of the type established in Germany has been absent in India thus far. For this reason, only related disciplines such as sociology, political science, labour market research and general pedagogics have looked at partial aspects within this area in the past. The approach has also tended to be sporadic, as the relevant publication status documents.

5.6 Procedures for quality assurance in vocational education and training

5.6.1 Quality assurance in vocational education and training

External research findings tend to paint a problematic picture of vocational education and training in India (Pilz et al. 2015a; 2015b; Tara et al. 2016). In the past, the quality of the Indian VET system has been an object of criticism in multiple regards, and this has also had an impact on the activities of foreign companies in India (Pilz/Li 2014b). An Efficiency Study Report on state ITIs in India produced by the International Labour Organization concluded that the employability of those competing programmes at state ITIs is very low and that only about 30 to 40 per cent of such persons are in employment (or self-employment) subsequent to their training (ILO 2003, p. 31).

In an investigation into the learning opportunities available to fishing families in the federal state of Orissa, Pilz/Wilmshöfer (2015c) concluded that the state ITIs were poorly equipped, were difficult to access because the distances involved were too long and failed to meet the needs of both those interested in pursuing training and the local labour market.

A further survey of cookshop operators in two Indian states also arrived at the finding that the formal training provision offered by state ITIs did not fulfil the requirements of those potentially interested in continuing training (Pilz et al. 2015 a).

A recent commission set up by the MSDE to investigate vocational education and training in general and the role of the Sector Skill Councils in particular also identified serious defects. It found that coordination of the various VET activities was inadequate and that vested interests dominated. The fact that the kind of bureaucracy that is in place in India overlaps in many places also hindered efficient management (Prasad 2016).

Against this background (see also previous chapter), a high degree of significance needs to be accorded to increasing and securing quality. This is also the reason why "One Nation One Standard" has become the mantra for quality assurance in vocational education and training. The aim is to ensure that national standards and the quality of qualifications gain international recognition in order to guarantee work opportunities at home and abroad for India's young people. The quality of training programmes is measured on the basis of competencies acquired and the employability of trainees. The following parameters have been identified for the purpose of improving quality:

▶ Quality assurance via integration into the NSQF
▶ Training programmes that are relevant to the labour market
▶ Recognition of prior knowledge
▶ Alignment of the curriculum
▶ National framework for certifications
▶ Employability skills
▶ Job placement (see MSDE 2015, p. 24)

However, quality assurance of vocational education and training programmes remains a work in progress. The MSDE is calling for all training measures in both general and vocational education to be aligned to the NSQF by 2018 (see Chapter 5.6.2). The objective is for certification of education and training programmes to take place via the stipulation of minimum standards. This will facilitate effective, generally valid, reliable, fair and transparent assessment within the scope of the NSQF. More precise details regarding the current status will be presented in the next chapter (MSDE 2015).

Academic research findings on the interpretation of quality and implementation of this in practice currently exist in only a very limited form. A study conducted by Tara et al. (2016) at least provides an initial insight. In 2014, interviews with the principals of state ITIs were carried out in the federal states of Karnataka, Orissa and Tamil Nadu and in New Delhi. A total of 15 cases were investigated. These varied both in terms of the size of the institutions and their location (rural/urban). The surveys of the school principals revealed that their understanding of quality was very strongly oriented towards output. The employability of persons completing the programmes and the satisfaction of stakeholders were viewed as the most important quality characteristics of vocational education and training at state ITIs. This interpretation is in line with the stipulations of the Indian government. Quality is associated with both output and outcome, i.e. the competencies and skills acquired by those completing the programmes and their opportunities on the labour market. By way of contrast, the process qualities of good teaching did not play a major part in the interviews conducted for the investigation.

5.6.2 National qualifications frameworks

Over the past few years, India has set itself the task of making competencies acquired measurable. The introduction of the first qualifications framework made the recognition of qualifications possible both nationally (29 federal states) and internationally. The qualifications frameworks that have been relevant since 2009 are presented below.

The National Vocational Qualification Framework (NVQF) was the first qualifications framework to be initiated when the NSAP was founded in 2009. It was developed in conjunction with the MoLE with the aim of achieving international comparability of vocational and educational qualifications. The Indian approach towards lifelong learning and continuing and higher training is an essential component of the NVQF. The NVQF focuses on the recognition of competencies in the organised and non-organised sector achieved via both formal and informal training processes, particularly learning in the workplace. The qualifications framework facilitates vertical mobility between vocational and academic education (see Singh/Duvekot 2013; Singh 1996; 2017).

In 2011, the National Vocational Education Qualification Framework (NVEQF) was introduced under the auspices of the MHRD. The objective was the creation of a "common reference framework for linking various vocational qualifications and setting common principles and guidelines for a nationally recognised qualifications system and standard" (Singh 2017, p. 109). The reason for adapting the NVQF (which applied up until this point) is the inclusion of pre-vocational provision in secondary and higher education.

A further updating of the qualifications framework took place in 2013. The goal of the Indian government was the integration of the NVQF and NVEQF into the current National Skills Qualification Framework (NSQF) as part of the India-EU Skills Development Project (Singh/Duvekot 2013). The national qualifications framework is outcomes- and competence-oriented. It summarises the various qualifications of an individual in accordance with skills and abilities. The NSQF provides comparability between general and vocational education and facilitates the transition from the informal to the organised sector (RPL) (see MSDE year of publication not stated, c). The NSQF consists of ten reference levels. Each level represents a different degree of complexity, knowledge and autonomy (see Table 34). The first level is the lowest of the reference levels. The individual stages contain criteria stating the learning outcomes defined in each case. The levels refer to competence achieved rather than to the time spent in a programme (see Table 34) (see MoF 2013).

One particular characteristic of the NSQF is that all types of competencies may be recognised, including ITI qualifications or qualifications gained by participants who terminate a programme prematurely. The international equivalence stated also makes global mobility easier for qualified workers from India (see MSDE year of publication not stated, c).

In order to facilitate better understanding, important components of the NSQF are described below (see MoF 2013).

National Occupational Standards (NOS) stipulate the performance level, knowledge and understanding of a certain task in the workplace. Each individual NOS defines a core competence for an occupation.

Qualification Packages (QP) describe a sum of several NOSs for a certain occupation. These QPs are in place for every sector and every occupation. The QPs form the basis both for the curriculum and for evaluation. The various performance levels in the respective occupation can be aligned to the NSQF.

Recognition of Prior Learning (RPL) is in some cases also referred to as Accreditation of Prior Learning. RPL is an instrument which facilitates the integration and assessment of competencies acquired in the non-organised sector within the formal educational system. This is a pioneering approach, especially in the Indian context, where more than 90 per cent of the labour demand are employed in the informal sector. The RPL instrument is outcome-oriented and capable of alignment to the NSQF. Evidence of competencies acquired cannot mostly be provided in the form of a certificate because such competencies were obtained by informal means. For this reason, a test procedure in which competencies are identified is used for categorisation in the NSQF. These test procedures have, for example, been successfully deployed in the MES programme (see Chapter 5.8). The Ministry of Tourism conducts aptitude tests and subsequently certifies the qualification of the participants. Determination of the qualification level in turn facilitates alignment to the NSQF (see MoF 2013; Mehrotra 2014).

Table 34: Extract from the NSQF

Level	Process required	Professional knowledge	Professional skill	Core skill	Responsibility
1	Prepares a person to carry out processes that are repetitive on a regular basis and require no previous practice	Familiar with common trade terminology, instructional words meaning and understanding	Routine and repetitive, takes account of safety and security measures	Reading and writing, addition and subtraction, personal financing, familiarity with social and religious diversity, hygiene and environment	No responsibility, always works under continuous instruction and close supervision
[...]					
5	Job that requires well-developed skill, with clear choice of procedures in a familiar context	Knowledge of facts, principles, processes and general concepts in a field of work or study	A range of cognitive and practical skills required to accomplish tasks and solve problems by selecting and applying basic methods, tools, materials and information	Desired mathematical skill, understanding of social, political topics and some skill of collecting and organising information, communication	Responsibility for own work and learning and some responsibility for others' work and learning
[...]					
9	Advanced knowledge and skill, critical understanding of the subject, demonstrating mastery and innovation, completion of substantial research and dissertation			Responsible for decision-making in complex technical activities involving unpredictable study/work situations	
10	Highly specialised knowledge and problem-solving skill to provide original contribution to knowledge through research and scholarship			Responsible for strategic decisions in unpredictable complex situations of work/study	

Source: MoF 2013, pp. 10 ff.

5.7 International mobility/internationalisation/international vocational education and training cooperation

5.7.1 Private sector

There are more than 3,000 German companies in India, various of which conduct vocational education and training based on German standards, and these are highly significant (see IHK year of publication not stated). Some of the best-known examples are the initiatives by the Gedee Technical Training Institute (GTTI) and by Bosch und Volkswagen.

The GTTI was established in Coimbatore in 2002 with the support of the Herzogenau-rach-based machine tool manufacturer G.D. Weiler and the Nuremberg Chamber of Commerce and Industry. It offers a range of training programmes in technical occupa-tions (such as mould- and toolmaker, welder, mechatronics technician etc.) at the high-est level. The institute is supported by Gedee Weiler (P) Ltd., G.D.W. Werkzeugmaschi-nen, UMS Technologies Ltd. and G-Plast (P) Ltd. German companies including Festo, Fanuc, Siemens, Keller, BF and WIM assist the GTTI with the provision of equipment and software (see GTTI year of publication not stated).

The Bosch Vocational Training Centre (BVTC) was founded in Bangalore as long ago as 1960. The provision offered by Bosch includes dual training in line with the German model at the locations of Pune, Jaipur and Bangalore. Trainees in the Bosch programme may enter three-year training under the ATS after completion of the tenth class (see Chapter 4.3.2). Selection of suitable candidates takes place on the basis of final school marks, a written test and an interview. Earnings opportunities during training are be-tween €40 and €54, significantly higher than in the state ATS. The curriculum is aligned to the requirements of the Indian training market. The Bosch training centres currently have more than 20 instructors. Two different programmes are offered. Trade Appren-ticeship Training provides two courses per cohort, each with 30 participants. Graduate Apprenticeship Training consists of one course per cohort, in which 30 places are avail-able (see Mehrotra et al. 2014).

Volkswagen (VW) is a further German training provider that is active in India. Since 2011, the company has been offering a vocational training programme within the scope of the ATS. The Volkswagen Academy Pune runs a three-and-a-half year course in "Mechanic Mechatronics" which ties in with the German dual system and follows a Ger-man-Indian curriculum. The training centre is state-recognised and has been accredited as a Basic Training Centre & Related Instructions (BTC & RI) by the Directorate of Voca-tional Education and Training (DVET)[16] and the NCVT. Participation in the programme requires completion of the tenth class, a written test, a skills test and a personal inter-view. Only 16 participants are admitted per cohort. The examination is conducted by the NCVT and the Association of German Chambers of Commerce and Industry (DIHK) via its foreign chamber of commerce in India (AHK) (Wessels 2012; VW 2016).

At this point, mention should be made of the fact that German companies in India do not merely offer extensive training measures. In many cases, depending on the field of activity and sector, they have also frequently designed highly flexible training meas-ures which range from brief induction programmes to safety training and may extend to encompass comprehensive specialist training measures (Pilz 2016; Pilz/Pierenkemper 2014a).

---

16   Only applies in the federal state of Maharashtra.

5.7.2 Multilateral institutions

Multilateral institutions such as the World Bank, the ILO, UNESCO and the OECD draw up joint strategies and programmes for economic policy and social cooperation with India. Two institutions and the cooperation agreements they have entered into in the field of vocational education and training will be presented as examples below.

The World Bank supports the NSDA in the evaluation of various Skill Development Programmes, including in Assam, Andhra Pradesh, Rajasthan, Madhya Pradesh and Odisha. The following vocational training programmes have received assistance from the World Bank (MoLE 2014):

▹ Aajeevika Skills, Ministry of Rural Development

▹ Skill Development Initiative Scheme (SDIS), MoLE

▹ Skill Training for Employment Promotion, Ministry of Housing and Urban Poverty Alleviation

▹ Training of partners for the NSDC Initiative

▹ Vocational Training Improvement Project (VTIP)

One example of the most important reforms realised in India by the World Bank is the establishment of Centres of Excellence as part of a process for the upgrading of conventional state ITIs (Rao et al. 2014, p. 43) (see Chapter 4.3.1). Another instance is the setting up of Institutional Management Committees (IMC) to foster the participation of private institutions within the scope of the PPP initiative for vocational education and training programmes. The World Bank made a major contribution towards the development of decentralised and private providers for apprenticeship training and funded the creation of Institutes for Training of Teachers (IToTs) in several federal states.

The ILO focuses on topics linked to the topics of quality, assessment and teacher training and on the NIOS programme (see Chapter 3.4.8). Recognition of Prior Learning (RPL) plays a particular role in this regard. The ILO provides particular assistance to persons with disabilities and also funds online-based learning programmes. In addition, it supports the Ajeevika National Rural Livelihood Mission (NRLM). The NRLM is a programme aimed at combating poverty which was launched in 2011 by the Ministry of Rural Development (MoRD).

Further to this, the ILO and the World Bank have instigated studies which have delivered an important impetus for vocational education and training research (see Chapter 5.5).

5.7.3 Indian think tanks

India has a number of institutes which are involved in looking at issues relating to the future. The three institutes described below are state bodies which are involved in aspects such as interdisciplinary research in the country.

The Central Staff Training and Research Institute (CSTARI) was founded in Calcutta in 1968 by the DGT in cooperation with the German Federal Government (GIZ 2013). CSTARI has been subject to the MSDE since April 2015. The remits of this institution for teacher training and teaching materials can be divided into three core areas. These are training, research and development. The programmes for which CSTARI is responsible are CTS and CoE (see Chapter 4.3.1), CITS (see Chapter 5.4.2) and MES (see Chapter 4.6)

Twelve courses were offered within the field of training during the year 2016/2017. The duration of these is between five and twelve days. The number of participants is usually restricted to 20. Only ten persons are admitted to the course in Training Methodology. Depending on the course, between four and eight dates are offered per year (CSTARI 2016) (see Table 35).

Table 35: Training provision in the 2016/2017 course year

No.	Course	Duration (days)	Number of participants
1	Assessors Competency Improvement Programme (ACIP)	5	20
2	Training for VTP Trainers (TVT)	5	20
3	Computer Application in Training (CAT)	12	20
4	Application and use of modern audiovisual aids (AVA)	5	20
5	Development of teaching & instructional skills (DTIS)	5	20
6	Employability skills (ES)	12	20
7	DGT officers induction programme (DOIP)	5	20
8	Management Development programme (MDP)	5	20
9	2D drafting using CAD software	12	20
10	Training Methodology	12	10
11	Instructional Methodology	12	20
12	English Communication Skills	5	20

Source: CSTARI 2016

Within the field of research, the focus is on the following areas (see ibid.):

▶ Feasibility studies for the introduction of new occupational fields under CTS/ATS

▶ Tracer studies, i.e. monitoring employment entered into by those completing ITI programmes

▷   Modernisation of state ITIs

▷   Skills analyses

▷   Stipulation of training requirements for disabled persons and other disadvantaged groups

▷   Planning and revision of spatial norms for vocational education and training programmes

▷   Stipulation of qualification requirements for trainers

In 2015, a total of 148 research projects was conducted and 119 curricula for various vocational education and training programmes were developed or revised.

In the field of development, teaching materials are drawn up and disseminated and courses are offered to ensure effective implementation of training programmes. In order to achieve these tasks, CSTARI is equipped with a model workshop, its own photo laboratory, an electronics laboratory and an internal print works (see ibid.).

The Central Instructional Media Institute (CIMI) in Chennai was opened in 1986 by the MoLE in cooperation with the GIZ (acting on behalf of the German Federal Government) (see GIZ 2013). This institute is responsible for various areas. It works in a similar way to CSTARI in making materials available to the CTS, the CoEs and MES, and it also offers train-the-trainer programmes. In addition, the CIMI takes charge of the translation of Instructional Media Packages (IMPs) into various regional languages. Further focuses are the continuing development of online learning tools and the provision of video-based learning programmes (see NIMI 2010).

The PSS Central Institute of Vocational Education (PSSCIVE) was founded in Bhopal in 1993 and named after Pandit Sunderlal Sharma, who devoted himself to sponsoring the needs of persons from Scheduled Castes and Scheduled Tribes in particular. The institute forms part of the NCERT (see Chapter 3.2), which is in turn subject to the MHRD. At the same time, it acts as a centre for UNESCO's International Project on Technical and Vocational Education (UNEVOC) (see PSSCIVE 2013).

The institute's vision is "to be a world class resource institution by providing research, development and training inputs for the development of vocational education and training and skilled human resource by 2020". Its mission is "to provide research, development and training to a wide spectrum of target groups so as to equip them with knowledge and skills and to prepare them for smooth transition from school to work." PSSCIVE is responsible for various core elements of vocational education and training at secondary schools. It advises and supports the MHRD and the state governments with regard to the implementation of VET programmes in accordance with the stipulations of the NSQF. It develops guidelines, competence-based curricula and teaching and learning materials for the secondary and upper secondary sectors. The institute's task area further encompasses the training of key persons (senior teachers and school principals). PSSCIVE also pursues research projects on current topics. The results of these are published in its own journal entitled "Indian Journal of Vocational Education (IJVE)" (PSS-CIVE 2016).

5.7.4 German education and training providers

There are many national and international education and training providers in India (see GOVET year of publication not stated). Two German stakeholders delivering various education and training programmes in India will be presented below.

Don Bosco or **Don Bosco Mondo** supports particularly disadvantaged children and young people. Its aim is to use education to combat poverty and promote development (Don Bosco Mondo year of publication not stated). Don Bosco[17] was the founder of the Salesian Society and began work in India as early as 1926. Today, 2,408 Salesians are active in 350 institutions. Institutions for street children and young people at risk extend as a network right across India and have a particular representation in rural educational development work amongst the indigenous tribes in the north-east of the country.

In 2013, the Indian education and training provider NIFE was taken over by the **TÜV Rheinland Technical Inspection Agency (TÜV Rheinland)**. The TÜV Rheinland NIFE Academy, which has been offering advanced vocational training courses in more than 70 sectors since 1992, plays an important role in the Skill Development Initiative. In 2015, a number of programmes in areas such as fire protection, lift technology and fibre optics were certified by the NSDC (see Chapter 5.8.2). This enables participants to obtain a bank credit and better employment opportunities across the whole of India (see TÜV Rheinland NIFE year of publication not stated).

5.7.5 German state agencies

German-Indian cooperation for sustainable economic, ecological and social development has been in place for many years. A multitude of joints projects has been instigated over the past 60 years. An increasing degree of significance is attached to cooperation in the field of research and education in particular. This was also revealed in the third German-Indian Government Consultations (2015), which included an agreement on cooperation within VET and also fostered an intensification of cooperation between institutes of higher education in the two countries (see BMBF year of publication not stated). Current projects and cooperation agreements between the various institutions are presented below.

Federal Ministry of Education and Research (BMBF) – under the lead management of the BMBF and within the scope of the German-Indian VET Working Group, BIBB has been engaging in close cooperation with the Indian government and with institutions

---

17   Member of the Missionaries of St. Francis de Sales.

and associations involved with vocational education and training since 2008. In October 2010, BIBB and iMOVE signed a cooperation agreement with the Federation of Indian Chambers of Commerce and Industry (FICCI). The FICCI is the oldest Indian chamber and industry association and has more than 80,000 member companies.

iMOVE – the BMBF initiative "International Marketing of Vocational Education" supports the internationalisation of initial and continuing vocational education and training services from Germany. The aim of iMOVE's activities in India is to create the best possible environment for the export of VET services. iMOVE markets German vocational education and training in India and advises German providers about the Indian market. For this purpose, work takes place at various levels with a diverse range of stakeholder groups. Cooperation with India is highly significant in terms of educational exports. The "iMOVE" brand has become successfully established amongst German and Indian partners via the presence of dedicated consultants and offices in the country (since October 2012). Within the scope of the German-Indian Working Group, an agreement was reached via the BMBF initiative to provide Indian trainers with training in Germany at the expense of the Indian government.

Association of German Chambers of Commerce and Industry (DIHK) – the BMBF is also funding the (further) establishment of eleven German chambers of commerce and industry abroad, including in India. The aim is to consolidate VET cooperation in India via the so-called VETnet project, which was launched in 2013. In October 2015, VETnet was extended for a further three years. The goal of the project is the implementation of dual elements in various training programmes. A pilot course in metalworking was instigated at the beginning of 2015 in cooperation with locally based companies, the Indo-German Chamber of Commerce (IGCC) and the Don Bosco ITI Pune. Because of rising demand, a one-year training programme in the occupation of industry mechanic started at the end of 2015. The next stage planned is to offer a one-year course in mechatronics for diploma holders via cooperation between the IGCC and the State Polytechnic in Pune.

Federal Ministry for Economic Cooperation and Development (BMZ) – in 2014 and at the start of 2015, the BMZ investigated the possibility of renewing its commitment to vocational education and training in India. Three integrated preliminary missions in 2014 and two further scrutiny visits in 2015 with the involvement of the BMBF and GOVET focused on conducting interviews with ministries, companies, training institutes, the Indo-German Chamber of Commerce, and various initial and continuing training providers. On this basis, the GIZ presented the BMZ with a three-year project schedule for India and was subsequently commissioned with the execution of this project (see BIBB year of publication not stated).

German Agency for International Cooperation (GIZ) – during the period from May 2014 to May 2015, the GIZ conducted preliminary missions and scrutiny visits in India on behalf of the BMZ (see above). The aim was the development of options for project activities in the field of vocational education and training in India. The BMBF was involved in the missions. In May 2016, this provided the foundations for the commissioning of a three-year project entitled Indo-German Programme for Vocational Education and Training (IGVET). The objective of the project is to work together on improving conditions for cooperative VET in India by creating a stronger degree of collaboration between the state and trade and industry. Total investment volume is €3 million. The project partner is the MSDE (GIZ 2016a). As a result, three main project focuses are currently being pursued in three areas. These comprise a cluster for automobile components in Aurangabad (Maharashtra), an electronics cluster in Bangalore (Karnataka) and a cluster for the construction sector in Bhiwadi (Rajasthan) (GIZ 2016b).

Thanks to support from the GIZ, a series of industry-related "tool rooms" had already been established in the past. Measures are taking place in some of these up to the present day, the main focus being on company-based continuing training. Alongside the tool rooms, which formed and still form part of technical training for skilled workers and master craftsmen, projects concentrating on teacher training and on the development of learning materials were also conducted (see Table 36).

sequa GmbH – from November 2010 to October 2013, sequa GmbH acted on behalf of the GIZ to deliver an "umbrella programme for the support of smaller companies in India" in the northern and central parts of the country. The aim of the project is to provide selected Indian chambers and associations with sustainable and requirements-oriented services for small firms and small and medium-sized companies. The plan is for the organisations of trade and industry to help create an improved services environment for these categories of company so as to enable them to increase income and employment. Raising competitiveness plays an important role in combating poverty in India. At the end of its term, the decision was taken that the project should be extended (see BIBB year of publication not stated).

Table 36: Summary of significant German-Indian projects funded by the GIZ in vocational education and training (1959–2010)

	Programme	State/federal state	Year
Technical training for skilled workers and master craftsmen	Prototype Training Centre (PTC)	Okhla (Delhi)	1958–1965
	Foreman Training Institute (FTI)	Bangalore/Tamil Nadu	1970–2001
	Central Tool Room (CTR)	Ludhiana/Punjab	1979–1995
	Tool Rooms	Lucknow/Uttar Pradesh, Ahmedabad/Gujarat, Indore/Madhya Pradesh, Aurangabad/Maharashtra	1992–1993 1987–2003
	Centre for Electronic Test Engineering (CETE)	Kolkata/West Bengal	1994–2008
	Society for Electronic Test Engineering (SETE)	Delhi, Bangalore/Tamil Nadu, Pune/Maharashtra, Hyderabad/Andhra Pradesh, Kolkata/West Bengal	2001–2005
	Polytechnic Unit (PDU)	Bhopal/Madhya Pradesh	1986–1997
	Centre for Research and Industrial Staff Performance (CRISP)	Bhopal/Madhya Pradesh	1997–2002
	Hi-Tech Training Scheme	Bangalore/Tamil Nadu	1995–2002
	Indo-German Institute of Advanced Technology (IGIAT)	Visakhapatnam/Andhra Pradesh	2005–2010
Teacher training – learning materials	Central Staff Training and Research Institute (CSTARI)	Kolkata/West Bengal	1968–1979
	Central Instructional Media Institute (CIMI)	Chennai/Tamil Nadu	1995–2004
Reform of vocational training (national)	National Vocational Training System (NVTS)	Delhi/national	1997–2004
	PISE	National	2004–2008

Source: GIZ 2013, p. 52

5.8 Major approaches to reform in vocational education and training

Over recent years, vocational education and training in India has been accorded a higher degree of significance in the country's educational policy. Several initiatives have been launched with a view to expanding occupational skills in light of the huge numbers of young people teeming onto the labour market and in the wake of the demands of industry, which is complaining of a serious shortage of skilled workers (British Council 2016). One of the tasks to be undertaken by the newly established Ministry of Development and Entrepreneurship (MSDE) (see Chapter 5.8.1) is the upgrading of the Indian system of vocational education and training. The MSDE is responsible for the training of workers right across the country and dedicates itself to a number of core areas. These are minimisation of the gulf between supply of and demand for skilled worker training, establishment of a training framework for VET and the enhancement and expansion of skills and competencies. The MSDE is supported in the setting of new standards by the National Skill Development Agency (NSDA), the NSDC, the National Skill Development Fund (NSDF), 38 Sector Skill Councils (SSC) and 187 training partners. The newly established ministry also intends to enter into alliances with bodies such as universities, NGOs, international organisations and, not least, local industry (see Pilz 2016a, p. 11).

One essential aim is the embedding of practical components into training. Pilz (2016) calls for a multi-stakeholder partnership, i.e. cooperation between all parties involved (public and private sectors companies, industry associations) in order to drive forward development in the field of TVET and provide long-term re-enforcement.

Figure 2: The ecological system of training measures in India

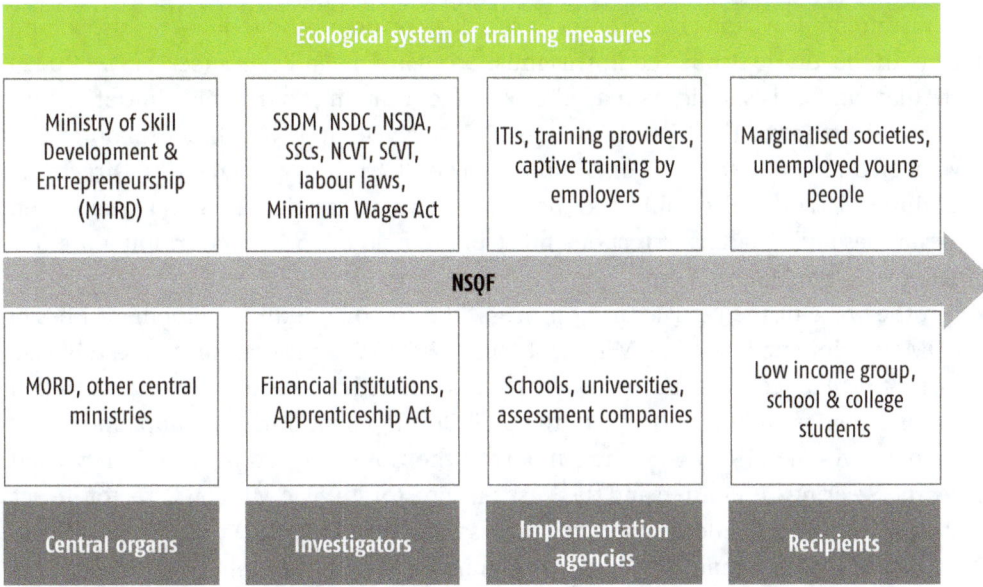

Source: FICCI/KPMG 2014, p. 15

The approaches towards reform being adopted in India are primarily concentrated on training/further training and on expanding the occupational skills and competencies of the Indian population. Within the scope of these endeavours, there is a multitude of competent bodies and programmes often exhibit duplications (see FICCI/KPMG 2014, p.16). The programmes initiated over recent years operate under differing general conditions with regard to funding criteria, duration of training, maximum number of participants, learning outcomes, monitoring and many other aspects besides. In order to achieve a better bundling and coordination of existing projects and new initiatives, Prime Minister Narendra Modi announced the establishment of the Ministry of Skill Development and Entrepreneurship (MSDE) in 2014 (see MSDE 2015). The system of the Indian Skill Development Programme is summarised in Figure 2 and presented in detail in the following sub-chapters.

5.8.1 Ministry of Skill Development and Entrepreneurship (MSDE)

The MSDE was founded in 2014. As already mentioned, the MSDE is responsible for the coordination of the various Skill Development Programmes and for the stipulation of norms. The norms for the different programmes encompass standards for input/ output, financing and costs, certification of third parties and costs incurred for evaluation. The remit assumed by the MSDE is that of a flexible coordinating agency which seeks to take account of the requirements of the 29 federal states and of the various social groups. Although the state governments are free to act at their own discretion in determining provisions in order to accord due consideration to local needs, compliance with the jointly stipulated norms must be ensured at all times (see MSDE 2015). Particular emphasis should be placed on the fact that all programmes initiated since the establishment of the MSDE, such as NSDA, NSDF and NSDC (see Chapter 5.1) have been bundled within this one ministry. The DGET, now renamed the Directorate of Training (DGT), is also subject to the MSDE. This means that all Skill Development Programmes and all areas of responsibility in the field of vocational training are now governed via the MSDE.

In the wake of the restructuring process, the National Skill Development Mission (NSDM) was initiated by Prime Minister Modi in 2015. This programme was established in order to create convergence between sectors and federal states with regard to joint training activities within the scope of the Skill Development Initiative. Implementation takes place via the MSDE with the support of the Governing Council for Policy Guidance, the Steering Committee and the Mission Directorate. The Mission Directorate acts as the executive organ and is supported in this function by the NSDA, the NSDC and the DGT. The institutions maintain direct communication with the state governments, and this facilitates effective management of the programme.

5.8.2 National Skill Development Corporation (NSDC)

The NSDC was instigated in 2009 as part of the National Skill Policy (NSP). The focus is on integration of the private sector within the context of the Public-Private Partnership (PPP) programme, to which reference has already been made. The overall aim of the NSDC is to provide training or continuing training to 500 million people by the year 2022 (see NSDC year of publication not stated). The NSDC makes a major contribution towards the achievement of this overarching target. Around 40 per cent of the Skill Initiative is delivered via NSDC training programmes and financial support. Expressed in terms of figures, this means providing training to 150 million people via an investment volume of €1.34 billion (see ibid.).

The NSDC has tied more than 211 training providers into the project. These providers have increased training volume within the institutions in order to be able to offer relevant short-term training programmes (see MSDE 2015).

Sector Skill Councils (SSCs) have been created for the purpose of bringing stakeholders together (industry, training providers and institutes of higher education). SSCs are responsible for occupational standards (QPs and NOS), the development of the competence framework (NSQF), provision of train-the-trainer programmes and for the execution of labour market studies. The specialist institutions also undertake assessment and certification of trainees pursuant to the National Occupational Standards (NOS) (see Chapter 5.6.2) (see MSDE 2016). Thirty-eight SCCs have been formed thus far, and council members include around 450 company representatives. Figure 3 illustrates the development of the SSCs over recent years. Although the creation of new core areas has increased year-on-year, the performance levels produced by these institutions thus far have been described as very ineffective (Prasad 2016).

Figure 3: Structure of the Sector Skill Councils (SSC)

	2010–11	2011–12	2012–13	2013–14	2014–15 & beyond
Priority Sector	• Auto • Retail • IT/ITeS	• Media and Entertainment • Healthcare • Gems & Jewellry • Leather • Electronics • BFSI	• Logistics • Construction • Food Processing	• Life Sciences • Hospitality • Textiles & Handlooms • Apparels • Handcrafts • Power • Iron & Steel	• Hydrocarbons • Management • Chemical & Petrochemicals • Strategic Manufacturing • Allied Manufacturing • Furniture & Furnishing • Education
Large Workforce		• Rubber	• Telecom • Capital Goods • Agriculture	• Aerospace & Aviation • Mining	• Sports • Paints & Coatings • Instrumentation
Informal Sectors	• Security		• Plumbing	• Beauty & Wellness	• Culture • Domestic Workers

* Approved in 2014–15

Source: MSDE year of publication not stated

5.8.3 Pradhan Mantri Kaushal Vikas Yojana (PMKVY)

PMKVY is a further programme within the scope of the Skill Development Initiative and was launched by the MSDE in 2015. The programme was instigated to train persons who have not received any formal training. The aim is for the training to facilitate entry to the labour market for young people in order to enable them to finance their own living costs and achieve social advancement. General institutional conditions are stipulated by the NSDC, the SCCs and the training providers. 1,976,087 young people have registered for the programme up until now. 1,973,299 successfully completed the programme, and 1,322,430 received certification for participation (see PMKVY 2016).

5.8.4 National Apprenticeship Promotion Scheme (NAPS)

The NAPS was initiated in August 2016 by the newly created MSDE. The programme supports the expansion and provision of training places. Around €1.34 billion has been made available for the scheme, the largest investment volume within the scope of the skill development endeavours undertaken over the past seven years. As already presented in Chapter 4.3.2, the ATS programme involves training that takes place in conjunction with local industry. 212,000 persons have currently completed a Trade Apprenticeship. The aim is to increase this figure to five million by 2020 (see iMOVE 2016). In order to create an incentive for companies, 25 per cent of training allowances are covered by the central government. This programme represents a completely new form of training measure in that financial inducements for companies are introduced for the first time. Alongside the financial support provided by the companies, the central government also offers a grant to cover 50 per cent of Broad Based Basic Training (BBBT) (see Chapter 4.3.1) (see DNA India 2016).

6 Literature

Agrawal, Tushar (2013): Vocational education and training programs (VET): An Asian perspective. Indira Gandhi Institute of Development Research (IGIDR).

Ahir, Kinjal V. (2015): Dropouts in School Education in India: Magnitude and Reasons. URL: https://www.worldwidejournals.com/paripex/file.php?val=May_2015_143 1776966__118.pdf [6 October 2017]

Ahmed, Tutan (2016): Socio-Economic Impact of VET: Are Students interested in Joining Vocational Education and Training in India: In the Context of Skilling Mission in India. In: Pilz, Matthias (ed.): India: Preparation for the World of Work – Education System and School to Work Transition. Springer VS, Wiesbaden, pp. 331–344.

AICTE (2015): All India Council for Technical Education – Approval Process Handbook 2015-2016. URL: http://www.aicte-india.org/downloads/Approval_Process_Handbook_2015_16.pdf [6 October 2017]

APEX Hi-Tech Institute (year of publication not stated): Trainers Training Programs. URL: http://www.apexhitechbangalore.in/faculties.html [6 October 2017]

Auswärtiges Amt *[Federal Foreign Office]* (2015): Indien *[India]*. URL: http://www.auswaertiges-amt.de/sid_8686C76428B5742043D3C59058C3F391/DE/Aussenpolitik/Laender/Laenderinfos/01-Nodes_Uebersichtsseiten/Indien_node.html [6 October 2017]

AWARE (2017): Homepage of Action for Welfare and Awakening in Rural Environment. URL: www.aware-group.com [6 October 2017]

Bhatnagar, Gaurav Vivek (2014): Delhi is now world's second most populous city. In: The Hindu, 12 July 2014. URL: http://www.thehindu.com/news/cities/Delhi/delhi-is-now-worlds-second-most-populous-city/article6203066.ece [6 October 2017]

BIBB (2015): Tarifliche Ausbildungsvergütung 2015 in Euro *[Training allowances based on collective wage agreements in euro]*. URL: https://www.bibb.de/dokumente/pdf/a21_ausbildungsverguetungen_2015.pdf [6 October 2017]

BIBB (year of publication not stated): Akteure der Berufsbildungszusammenarbeit in Indien *[Stakeholders of VET cooperation in India]*. URL: https://www.bibb.de/govet/de/10050.php [6 October 2017]

BMBF (year of publication not stated): Deutschland und Indien: Partner in Bildung und Forschung *[Germany and India – partners in education and research]*. URL: https://www.bmbf.de/de/deutschland-und-indien-partner-in-bildung-und-forschung-472.html [6 October 2017]

Bpb (2007): Neues Selbstbewusstsein und anhaltende Unterdrückung – Frauen in Indien *[New self-confidence and ongoing oppression – women in India]*. URL: http://www.bpb.de/internationales/asien/indien/44429/frauen-in-indien [6 October 2017]

Bpb (2014a): Große Armut und zunehmende Ungleichheit *[Great poverty and increasing inequality]*. URL: http://www.bpb.de/internationales/asien/indien/189202/grosse-armut-und-zunehmende-ungleichheit [6 October 2017]

Bpb (2014b): Kaste und Kastensystem in Indien *[Caste and caste system in India]*. URL: http://www.bpb.de/internationales/asien/indien/44414/kastenwesen [6 October 2017]

Bpb (2014c): Wirtschaftssystem und wirtschaftliche Entwicklung in Indien - Einführung und Überblick *[Economic system and economic development in India – introduction and summary]*. URL: http://www.bpb.de/internationales/asien/indien/44512/ueberblick-wirtschaft [6 October 2017]

Bpb (2015): Politik *[Policy]*. URL: http://www.bpb.de/internationales/asien/indien/44442/politik [6 October 2017]

British Council (2016), Overview of Indias's evolving skill development landscape. British Council India: New Delhi.

CBSE (2015): Senior School Curriculum 2015–16. Volume 1. URL: http://cbseacademic.in/web_material/Curriculum/SrSecondary/2015%E2%80%9316_Senior%20School%20Curriculum%20Volume%201.pdf [6 October 2017]

CEDEFOP (2009): European guidelines for validating non-formal and informal learning. Office for Official Publications of the European Communities, Luxembourg.

Chandra, Ramesh (2003): Encyclopaedia of Education in South Asia. Delhi.

Cheney, Gretchen Rhines; Ruzzi, Betsy Brown; Muralidharan, Karthik (2005): A profile of the Indian Education System. URL: http://www.teindia.nic.in/files/articles/indian_education_sysytem_by_karthik_murlidharan.pdf [6 October 2017]

CII and PwC (2013): Handbook on Corporate Social Responsibility in India. URL: https://www.pwc.in/assets/pdfs/publications/2013/handbook-on-corporate-social-responsibility-in-india.pdf [13 October 2017]

Clemens, Iris; Holzwarth, Simone (2009): Mit Bildung in die 'Flat World'? Bildung in Indien zwischen Reproduktion sozialer Strukturen und Transformation kultureller Tradierung *[Education as the route to the "flat world"? Education in India between the reproduction of social structures and the transformation of cultural tradition]* In: Internationales Asienforum *[International Asia Forum]*, Vol. 40, No. 1–2, pp. 39–58.

CSTARI (2016): Homepage Central Staff Training and Research Institute. URL: http://cstaricalcutta.gov.in [6 October 2017]

Debroy, Bibek; Tellis, Ashley J.; Trevor, Reece (ed.): Getting India Back on Track. An Action Agenda for Reform, Washington, D.C. 2014

Destatis (2015): Basistabelle der Erwerbsquote weltweit *[Basic table for the labour demand rate worldwide]*. URL: https://www.destatis.de/DE/ZahlenFakten/Laender-Regionen/Internationales/Thema/Tabellen/Basistabelle_Erwerbstaetige.html [6 October 2017]

Destatis (2017): Indien *[India]*. URL: https://www.destatis.de/DE/Publikationen/Thematisch/Internationales/Laenderprofile/Indien2017.pdf;jsessionid=37BE5671B4D-942620528202FAAE13E3A.cae1?__blob=publicationFile [6 October 2017]

DGT (2011): Recognition of multi-skilling courses offered in ITI upgrades as Centres of Excellence (CoE). URL: http://dget.nic.in/upload/uploadfiles/files/lettertoRailwayBoard_%20recognitionofmultiskillingcourses.pdf [6 October 2017]

DGT (2014a): Introduction – Upgraduation of 1,396 Govt. ITIs through PPP. URL: http://www.dget.nic.in/content/innerpage/introduction.php [6 October 2017]

DGT (2014b): Institutes for Training of Trainers (IToTs). URL: http://www.dget.nic.in/content/institute/institutes-for-training-of-trainers-itots.php [6 October 2017]

DGT (2014c): Skill Development Initiative Scheme (SDIS). URL: http://www.dget.nic.in/content/innerpage/introduction-sdis.php [6 October 2017]

DGT (2014d): Central Training Institute for Instructors. URL: http://www.dget.nic.in/content/institute/cti-chennai.php [6 October 2017]

DGT (2014e): Functions of the Directorate General. URL: http://dget.nic.in/content/innerpage/functions-of-the-directorate-general.php [6 October 2017]

DGT (2014f): National Vocational Training System in India. URL: http://dget.nic.in/upload/uploadfiles/files/task_responsebility.pdf [6 October 2017]

DGT (2014g): Admission for Training of Craft Instructors. URL: http://www.dget.nic.in/content/institute/admission--cti-chennai.php [6 October 2017]

DGT (2014h): Apex Hi-Tech Institute (AHI). URL: http://www.dget.nic.in/content/institute/apex-hi-tech-institute-ahi.php [6 October 2017]

DGT (2015a): Training - Broad Based Basic Training (BBBT). URL: http://dget.nic.in/content/institute/training-haldwani.php [6 October 2017]

DGT (2015b): Competency Based Curriculum for the Trade of Turner under CTS. URL: http://dget.nic.in/content/innerpage/trade-syllabus.php [6 October 2017]

DGT (2015c): Women Training. URL: http://dget.nic.in/content/institute/overview-wt.php [6 October 2017]

DGT (2015d): Key statistics. URL: http://www.dget.nic.in/content/institute/key-statistics.php [6 October 2017]

DGT (2015e): An overview of the Apprenticeship Training Scheme. URL: http://www.dget.nic.in/content/innerpage/overview-apprenticeship-training-scheme.php [6 October 2017]

DGT (2015f): An overview of the Craft Instructor Training Scheme (CITS). URL: http://www.dget.nic.in/content/innerpage/overview-cits.php [6 October 2017]

DNA India (2016): Cabinet approves the National Apprenticeship Promotion Scheme. Article dated 5 July 2016. URL: http://www.dnaindia.com/money/report-cabinet-approves-the-national-apprenticeship-promotion-scheme-2231502 [6 October 2017]

Don Bosco Mondo (year of publication not stated): Homepage Don Bosco Mondo. URL: http://www.don-bosco-mondo.de/hilfsprojekte/projektlaender/asien/indien/ [6 October 2017]

Economic Times (2015): Top 75 companies spent Rs. 4,000 crore on CSR 2015. Article dated 3 September 2015. URL: http://economictimes.indiatimes.com/news/company/corporate-trends/top-75-companies-spent-rs-4000-crore-on-csr-in-2015/articleshow/48781453.cms [6 October 2017]

FICCI (2006): FICCI Survey on 'The state of Industrial Training Institutes in India', New Delhi.

FICCI (2010): The Skill Development Landscape in India and Implementing Quality Skills Training. ICRA Management Consulting Services Limited (ed.). URL: http://www.ficci.com/SPdocument/20073/IMaCS.pdf [6 October 2017]

FICCI; KPMG (2014): Skilling India – A look back at the progress, challenges and the way forward. URL: http://ficci.in/spdocument/20405/FICCI-KPMG-Global-Skills-report.pdf [6 October 2017]

FTI (2016): Foreman Training Institute Bangalore. URL: http://www.ftibangalore.gov.in/index.html [6 October 2017]

Gengaiah, Uma (2016): NGO Initiatives: Non-Governmental Organisations Initiatives. In: Pilz, Matthias (ed.): India: Preparation for the World of Work – Education System and School to Work Transition. Springer VS, Wiesbaden, pp. 211–230.

GIZ (2013): The Energy and Resource Institute (TERI), New Delhi. URL: http://www.teriin.org [6 October 2017]

GIZ (2016a): Projektdaten Indien *[Project data India]*. URL: https://www.giz.de/projektdaten/index.action?request_locale=de_DE#?region=2&countries=IN [6 October 2017]

GIZ (2016b): Indo-German Programme for Vocational Education and Training (IGVET), New Delhi.

Goel, Vijay P. (2009): Technical and Vocational Education and Training (TVET) System/In India for Sustainable Development. MHRD.

GoI (2015): National Policy for Skill Development and Entrepreneurship 2015. Ministry of Skill Development and Entrepreneurship. URL: https://www.bibb.de/dokumente/pdf/Policy_Booklet_V2(2).pdf. [6 October 2017].

GOVET (year of publication not stated): GOVET Homepage. URL: https://www.bibb.de/govet/de/index.php [6 October 2017]

GTAI (2015): Lohn- und Lohnnebenkosten Indien *[Wage costs and ancillary wage costs in India]*. URL: https://www.giessen-friedberg.ihk.de/blob/giihk24/Geschaeftsbereiche/International/Nachrichten_Aussenwirtschaft/Newsletter/Internationale_Neuigkeiten/downloads/1838024/0f73cc20b86d9929441be685b945b8e8/Lohn_und_Lohnnebenkosten_in_Indien-data.pdf [6 October 2017]

GTAI (2016): Wirtschaftsdaten kompakt Indien *[Compact economic data on India]*. URL: https://www.gtai.de/GTAI/Content/DE/Trade/Fachdaten/MKT/2016/11/mkt201611222018_159630_wirtschaftsdaten-kompakt---indien.pdf?v=1 [6 October 2017]

GTTI (year of publication not stated): Homepage of GTTI. URL: http://www.gttiinfo.com/ [6 October 2017]

Gupta, Amita (2007): Schooling in India. In: Gupta, Amita [Ed.]: Going to school in South Asia. Greenwood Press. Westport/London, pp. 66–111.

Gupta, M. Sen (2009): Early Childhood Care and Education. PHI Learning Private Limited. New Delhi.

Gupta, Vishal; Raman, Charanya; Krisanthan, Balasundaram (2016): Secondary (9–10) and Higher Secondary (11–12) Education: Preparation for the World of Work: Secondary and Higher Secondary Education in India. In: Pilz, Matthias (ed.): India: Preparation for the World of Work – Education System and School to Work Transition. Springer VS, Wiesbaden, pp. 41–64.

Hahn, Karola (2005): Länderanalyse Indien – Der indische Markt für Hochschulbildung *[Country analysis of India – the Indian higher education market]*. Study conducted on behalf of the German Academic Exchange Service (DAAD). July/August 2005.

Hardgrave, Robert L.; Kochanek, Stanley A.: India. Government and Politics in a Developing Nation, Boston 2008

IAMR Survey (2010). In: Mehrotra, Santosh (2014): India's Skills Challenge. Oxford University Press, p. 105.

IHK (year of publication not stated): Länderinfo Indien *[Country information on India]*. URL: http://www.frankfurt-main.ihk.de/international/auslandsmaerkte/laender-kontakte/g-k/indien/ [6 October 2017]

ILO (2003): Industrial Training Institutes of India: The Efficiency Study Report. Subregional Office for South Asia, ILO, New Delhi.

Imhasly, Bernard (2015): Indien – Ein Länderporträt *[India – a country portrait]*. Bundeszentrale für politische Bildung *[Federal Agency for Civic Education]*. Volume 1564. Bonn.

iMOVE (2016): Indische Regierung investiert in Kompetenzentwicklung *[Indian government invests in competence development]*. Article dated 3 August 2016. URL: http://www.imove-germany.de/cps/rde/xchg/imove_projekt_de/hs.xsl/alle_news.htm?content-url=/cps/rde/xchg/imove_projekt_de/hs.xsl/27795.htm [6 October 2017]

ITI Bhavnagar (2005): Upgradation of ITIs into Centres of Excellence – Broad guidelines for implementation of the Broad Based Basic Training in Automobiles Sector. URL: http://www.itibhavnagar.org/AutomobileBBBT.pdf [6 October 2017]

Joshi, Shachi; Pandey, Gayatri.; Sahoo, Bimal K. (2014): Comparing Public and Private Vocational Training Providers. In: Mehrotra, Santosh (ed.), India's Skills Challenge:

reforming vocational education and training to harness the demographic dividend. New Delhi, pp. 86–128.

Jung, Stefanie; Pilz, Matthias (2016): Skillerwerb im informellen Sektor: Das Beispiel von Ananasfarmern im Nord-Osten Indiens *[Skill acquisition in the informal sector – the example of pineapple farmers in north-east India]*. In: Kölner Zeitschrift für Wirtschaft und Pädagogik *[Cologne Journal of Business and Education]*, Vol. 31, Issue 61, pp. 82–104.

Khare, Mona (2016): Higher Education/University: Taking the Skills March Forward in India – Transitioning to the World of Work. In: Pilz, Matthias (ed.): India: Preparation for the World of Work – Education System and School to Work transition. Springer VS, Wiesbaden, pp. 103-140.

Kooperation International (2015): Indien *[India]*. URL: http://www.kooperation-international.de/buf/indien.html [6 October 2017]

KPMG (2015): India's CSR reporting survey 2015. URL: https://home.kpmg.com/in/en/home/insights/2015/12/indias-csr-reporting-survey.html [6 October 2017]

Krisanthan, Balasundaram; Pilz, Matthias (2014): Vorberufliche Bildung in Indien – Eine Analyse der curricularen Verankerung und der schulischen Praxis *[Pre-vocational education in India – an analysis of curricular establishment and school practice]*. In: Tertium Comparationis – Journal für International und Interkulturell Vergleichende Erziehungswissenschaft *[Tertium Comparationis – Journal of Internationally and Interculturally Comparative Educational Science]*, Vol. 20, Issue 1, pp. 61–80.

Länderdaten Info (2015): Vergleich weltweiter Lebenshaltungskosten *[Comparison of worldwide costs of living]*. URL: https://www.laenderdaten.info/lebenshaltungskosten.php [6 October 2017]

Lang-Wojtasik, Gregor (2013): Das Bildungssystem in Indien *[The educational system in India]*. In: Adick, Christel [Ed.]: Bildungsentwicklungen und Schulsysteme in Afrika, Asien, Lateinamerika und der Karibik *[Educational developments and school systems in Africa, Asia, Latin America and the Caribbean]*. Münster [and others]: Waxmann, pp. 213–231.

Majumdar, Shyamal (2008): Workforce Development in India, Policies and Practices. The Asian Development Bank Institute (ADBI), URL: https://www.adb.org/sites/default/files/publication/159351/adbi-workforce-dev-india.pdf [6 October 2017]

Männicke, Jürgen (2011): Marktstudie Indien für den Export beruflicher Aus- und Weiterbildung *[Market study of India for the export of initial and continuing training]*. iMOVE at the Federal Institute for Vocational Education and Training (ed.), 2nd revised edition, May 2011, Bonn. URL: https://www.imove-germany.de/cps/rde/xbcr/imove_projekt_de/d_iMOVE-Marktstudie_Indien_2011.pdf [6 October 2017]

Mehrotra, Santosh (2014): India's Skills Challenge. Oxford University Press.

Mehrotra, Santosh et al. (2014): Vocational Education and Training Reform in India Business Needs in India and Lessons to be Learned from Germany. Bertelsmann

Stiftung. URL: https://www.bertelsmann-stiftung.de/fileadmin/files/BSt/Publika-tionen/GrauePublikationen/GP_Vocational_Education_and_Training_Reform_in_India.pdf [6 October 2017]

Mehrotra, Santosh et al. (2015): Vocational Training in India and the duality principle: A case for evidence-based reform. In: PROSPECTS, Vol. 45, Issue 2, pp. 259–273. URL: http://link.springer.com/article/10.1007/s11125-015-9358-x [6 October 2017]

MHRD (2012): National Vocational Education Qualifications Framework (NVEQF). URL: http://mhrd.gov.in/nveqf [6 October 2017]

MHRD (2014): Education at a Glance. URL: http://mhrd.gov.in/sites/upload_files/mhrd/files/statistics/EAG2014_0.pdf [6 October 2017]

MHRD (2015a): Right to Education. URL: http://mhrd.gov.in/rte [6 October 2017]

MHRD (2015b): Apprentices Act, 1961. URL: http://mhrd.gov.in/sites/upload_files/mhrd/files/upload_document/ApprenticeAct1961.pdf [6 October 2017]

MHRD (2016a): Vocationalisation of Secondary Education. URL: http://mhrd.gov.in/vocationalisation [6 October 2017]

MHRD (2016b): Schemes of Technical Education. URL: http://mhrd.gov.in/techni-cal-education-13 [6 October 2017]

MHRD (2016c): University and Higher Education. URL: http://mhrd.gov.in/universi-ty-and-higher-education [6 October 2017]

MHRD (2016d): Educational Statistics at a Glance. URL: http://mhrd.gov.in/sites/up-load_files/mhrd/files/statistics/ESG2016_0.pdf [6 October 2017]

MHRD (2016e): All India Survey on Higher Education (2015–16). Ministry of Human Resource Development Department of Higher Education. New Delhi. URL: http://mhrd.gov.in/sites/upload_files/mhrd/files/statistics/AISHE2015-16.pdf [6 Octo-ber 2017]

MHRD (2016f): Cost and Equity in Accessing Secondary Education. URL: http://rmsaindia.gov.in/administrator/components/com_pdf/pdf/21af998405dd8a-494c543a3934098347-Cost-and-Equity-in-Accessing-Secondary-Education.pdf [6 October 2017]

MHRD (year of publication not stated): Ministry of Human Resource Development. URL: www.mhrd.gov.in [6 October 2017]

MoF (2013): NSQF Notification. In: Gazette of India. URL: http://mhrd.gov.in/sites/upload_files/mhrd/files/upload_document/NSQF-NOTIFICATION.pdf [6 October 2017]

MoLE (2014): Annual Report 2013–14. Government of India. URL: http://www.dget.nic.in/upload/uploadfiles/files/annualReport13-14.pdf [6 October 2017]

Mond, Marie; Pilz, Matthias (2011): Das Berufsbildungssystem in Indien: Heraus-forderungen und Lösungsansätze [The vocational education and training system in

India – challenges and possible solutions]. In: Hdb. d. Aus- und Weiterbildung *[Hand-book of Initial and Continuing Training]* update 218, July 2011.

MSDE (2015): National Policy for Skill Development and Entrepreneurship. URL: https://www.bibb.de/dokumente/pdf/Policy_Booklet_V2(2).pdf [6 October 2017]

MSDE (2016): QPs and NOS. URL: http://www.skilldevelopment.gov.in/qp&nos.html [6 October 2017]

MSDE (year of publication not stated, a): Sector Skill Councils (SSC). URL: http://msde.gov.in/ssc.html [6 October 2017]

MSDE (year of publication not stated, b): National Skill Development Mission. URL: http://msde.gov.in/nationalskillmission.html [6 October 2017]

MSDE (year of publication not stated, c): National Skills Qualifications Framework (NSQF). URL: http://msde.gov.in/nsqf.html [6 October 2017]

NATS (2013): Annual Report 2012–13. National Apprenticeship Training Scheme (NATS). URL: http://www.mhrdnats.gov.in/sites/default/files/SR%20_Annual%20Report.pdf [6 October 2017]

NCERT (2005): National Curriculum Framework. URL: www.ncert.nic.in/rightside/links/pdf/framework/english/nf2005.pdf [6 October 2017]

NCVT (year of publication not stated): Homepage of NCVT-Management Information System. URL: https://ncvtmis.gov.in/Pages/Home.aspx [6 October 2017]

NGO India (year of publication not stated): NGO Registration Methods. URL: http://www.ngosindia.com/resources/ngo_registration.php [6 October 2017]

NIMI (2010): A Brief Presentation on National Instructional Media Institute. URL: http://siteresources.worldbank.org/EDUCATION/Resources/278200-11217032 74255/1439264-1242337549970/6124382-1291074275592/7586048-129107 4664317/Nov11pm2NIMIPresentation.pdf [6 October 2017]

NIOS (year of publication not stated): Homepage National Institute of Open Schooling. URL: http://www.nios.ac.in [6 October 2017].

Norric (2006): Report on the System of Education in India. Nordic Recognition Information Centres. URL: http://norric.org/files/education-systems/India-2006.pdf [6 October 2017]

NSDC (2012): Infrastructure Sector Report, Talent Projections & Skills Gap Analysis (2022). Government of India. URL: http://www.nsdcindia.org/sites/default/files/files/infrastructure-report-2009.pdf [6 October 2017]

NSDC (year of publication not stated): Need Assessment Report on Building Trainers' Skills in Vocational Employability. New Delhi. URL: http://www.nsdcindia.org/sites/default/files/files/building-trainers-skills.pdf [6 October 2017]

Overwien, Bernd (2000): Informal Learning and the role of social movements. In: International Review of Education 46 (6), pp. 621–640.

Pillay, Hitendra (2014): India's Vocational Education Capacity to support the anticipated economic growth. Queensland University for Technology. April 2014.

Pilz, Matthias (2016), Training patterns of German companies in India, China, Japan and the USA: what really works? In: International Journal for Research in Vocational Education and Training, Vol. 3, Nr. 2, p. 66-87

Pilz, Matthias (2016a): India: Preparation for the World of Work – Education System and School to Work transition. Springer VS, Wiesbaden.

Pilz, Matthias (2016b): Typologies in comparative vocational education: Existing models and a new approach. In: Vocations and Learning, Volume 9, Issue 3, pp. 295–314.

Pilz, Matthias (2016c): Santosh Mehrotra - India's skills challenge: reforming vocational education and training to harness the demographic dividend [review]. In: Journal of Vocational Education and Training, Vol. 68, No. 2, pp. 280–281.

Pilz, Matthias (2016d): A View from the Outside: India's School to Work Transition Challenge – Strengths and Weakness. In: Pilz, Matthias (ed.): India: Preparation for the World of Work – Education System and School to Work transition. Springer VS, Wiesbaden. pp. 345–358.

Pilz, Matthias; Becker, Verena; Pierenkemper, Sarah (2015b): Berufsbildung in Indien: Herausforderungen zwischen Quantität und Qualität [*Vocational education and training in India – challenges between quantity and quality*]. In: Zeitschrift für Berufs- und Wirtschaftspädagogik [*Journal of Vocational and Business Education*], Vol. 111, Issue 4, pp. 502–523.

Pilz, Matthias; Li, Junmin (2014b): Tracing Teutonic footprints in VET around the world? – The skills development strategies of German companies in the USA, China and India. In: European Journal of Training and Development, 38 (8), pp. 745–763.

Pilz, Matthias; Pierenkemper, Sarah (2014a): Apprenticeship Programs – Lessons from Germany & German Companies in India. In: The Indian Journal of Industrial Relations: A Review of Economic & Social Development (IJIR), Vol. 49, No. 3, pp. 389–400.

Pilz, Matthias; Uma, Gengaiah; Venkatram, Rengan (2015a): Skills development in the informal sector in India: The case of street food vendors. In: International Review of Education, April 2015, Volume 61, Issue 2, pp. 191–209.

Pilz, Matthias; Wilmshöfer, Simon (2015c): The challenges of formal, non-formal and informal learning in rural India: the case of fishing families on the Chilika Lagoon, Orissa. In: PROSPECTS: Quarterly Review of Comparative Education, 45 (2), pp. 231–243.

Planning Commission (2008): Eleventh Five Year Plan. Vol. 1. New Delhi. URL: http://planningcommission.nic.in/plans/planrel/fiveyr/11th/11_v1/11th_vol1.pdf [6 October 2017]

Planning Commission (2013): Twelfth Five Year Plan. New Delhi. URL: http://planningcommission.nic.in/plans/planrel/fiveyr/12th/pdf/12fyp_vol3.pdf [6 October 2017]

Planning Commission (2014): Skill Development and Training Programmes of Central governments. URL: http://planningcommission.nic.in/reports/genrep/skilldev/rep_skilldev8.pdf [6 October 2017]

PMKVY (2016): Homepage Pradhan Mantri Kaushal Vikas Yojana. URL: http://pmkvy-official.org/Index.aspx [6 October 2017]

Prasad, Shri Sharda (2016): Report of the Committee for rationalization & optimization of the functioning of the Sector Skill Councils, Volume I, Ministry of Skill Development and Entrepreneurship, New Delhi.

Pratham (2015): Annual Status of Education Report (rural) 2014. ASER 2014.

PRS Legislative Research (2016): The Apprentices (Amendment) Bill, 2014. URL: http://www.prsindia.org/billtrack/the-apprentices-amendment-bill-2014-3354/ [6 October 2017]

PSSCIVE (2013): Homepage of PSSCIVE. URL: http://www.psscive.nic.in/ [12 September 2016, website was uploaded]

Ramasamy, Muthuveeran (2016): Demand-Driven Approaches in Vocational Education and Training: A Case Study of Rural Population in South India. Springer VS, Wiesbaden.

Ramasamy, Muthuveeran; Mani, Chandrakumar (2016): Company Training, Initial Training: Initial In-Company Vocational Training in India: Implications and Challenges for Indian Companies. In: Pilz, Matthias (ed.): India: Preparation for the World of Work – Education System and School to Work Transition. Springer VS, Wiesbaden, pp. 169–182.

Rao, K. S.; Sahoo, Bimal K.; Ghosh, Deboshree (2014): The Indian Vocational Education and Training System – An Overview. In: Mehrotra, Santosh (ed.): The Skills Challenge. Oxford University Press, pp. 37–85.

Sahni, Urvashi (2015): Primary Education in India: Progress and Challenges. In: The Second Modi-Obama Summit: Building the India-U.S. Partnership, pp. 35–38.

Singh, Madhu (1998): Curricular implications of competency requirement and utilization among small producers in New Delhi. In: Buchert, Lene [Ed.], Education reform in the South in the 1990s, Paris, UNESCO, p. 245-267

Singh, Madhu (2002): Adult Education in Selected Countries in the Asian Region – A reference for Politics, Programmes and Delivery Modes. UNESCO Institute for Education, Hamburg.

Singh, Madhu (2012): India's National Skills Development Policy and Implications for TVET and Lifelong Learning. In: Pilz, Matthias [ed.]: The Future of Vocational Education and Training in a Changing World. Wiesbaden, Springer, p. 179–211

Singh, Madhu (2017): National Qualifications Frameworks (NQF) and Support for Alternative Transition Routes for Young People. In: Pilz, Matthias (ed.): Vocational Education and Training in Times of Economic Crisis: Lessons from Around the World. Cham, Springer International, Cham. pp. 3–23.

Singh, Madhu; Duvekot, Ruud (2013): Linking Recognition Practices and National Qualifications Frameworks. UNESCO Institute for Lifelong Learning, Hamburg.

Singh, Ram Lakhan (2013): The NVQF and skills recognition. In: Singh, Madhu; Duvekot, Ruud (eds.): Linking Recognition Practices and National Qualifications Frameworks. UNESCO Institute for Lifelong Learning, Hamburg.

Sodhi, Joginder Singh (2014): India: Education System and School to Work Transition. In: Kölner Zeitschrift für Wirtschaft und Pädagogik *[Cologne Journal of Business and Education]*, Vol. 29, No. 56, pp. 57–78.

Sodhi, Joginder Singh; Wessels, Antje (2016): Informal Learning: Education and Skill Development in India's Informal Sector. In: Pilz, Matthias (ed.): India: Preparation for the World of Work – Education System and School to Work Transition. Springer VS, Wiesbaden. pp. 261–280.

Tara, S. Nayana; Kumar, N.S. Sanath (2016): Primary and Upper Primary Education (1-8): Initiative for the World of Work at the Primary and Upper Primary Education in India. In: Pilz, Matthias (ed.): India: Preparation for the World of Work – Education System and School to Work Transition. Springer VS, Wiesbaden, pp. 25–40.

Tara, S. Nayana; Kumar, N.S. Sanath (2017): Initiatives in Skill Upgrading: The Case of Centres of Excellence (COE) in Industrial Training Institutes (ITI) in Karnataka, India. In: Pilz, Matthias (ed.): Vocational Education and Training in Times of Economic Crisis: Lessons from Around the World. Cham, Springer International, Cham, pp. 151–170.

Tara, S. Nayana; Kumar, N.S. Sanath; Pilz, Matthias (2016): Quality of VET in India: The case of Industrial Training Institutes. In: TVET@asia, Issue 7, pp. 1–17. URL: http://www.tvet-online.asia/issue7/tara_etal_tvet7.pdf [6 October 2017]

TÜV Rheinland NIFE (year of publication not stated): Homepage of TÜV Rheinland NIFE. URL: http://www.nifeindia.com/index.php [6 October 2017]

UGC (2015): Guidelines for Introduction of Bachelor of Vocation (B. Voc.) Programme on universities and colleges under the National Skills Qualifications Framework (NSQF). URL: http://www.ugc.ac.in/pdfnews/8508026_Guidelines-on-B-Voc_Final.pdf [6 October 2017]

UN DESA (year of publication not stated): Indien: Durchschnittsalter der Bevölkerung von 1950 bis 2015 (Altersmedian in Jahren) *[India – average age of population from 1950 to 2015 (mean age in years)]*. URL: http://de.statista.com/statistik/daten/studie/200678/umfrage/durchschnittsalter-der-bevoelkerung-in-indien/ [6 October 2017]

Venkatram, Rengan (2016): (Technical) Colleges: Technical Education in India – The Strengths and Challenges. In: Pilz, Matthias (ed.): India: Preparation for the World of Work – Education System and School to Work Transition. Springer VS, Wiesbaden, pp. 81–102.

Venkatram, Rengan (2012): Vocational Education and training system (VET) in India. In: Pilz, Matthias [ed.]: The Future of Vocational Education and Training in a Changing World, Wiesbaden, Springer, p. 171–178

Vermeer, Manuel; Neumann, Clas (2015): Praxishandbuch Indien – Wie Sie Ihr Indiengeschäft erfolgreich managen *[Practical Handbook India—how to manage your Indian business successfully]*. 2nd updated edition. Springer Gabler, Wiesbaden.

VETnet (2016): Broschüre der AHK Indien *[Brochure of the German chambers of commerce and industry in India]*.

VW (2016): About Apprenticeship Programme. Brochure.

Wessels, Antje (2012): Das indische Berufsbildungssystem unter besonderer Berücksichtigung der Diversity-Frage *[The Indian VET system with special consideration of the diversity issue]*. GRIN Verlag, Munich.

Wessels, Antje; Pilz, Matthias (2016): Die Berufsbildung in Indien *[Vocational education and training in India]*. In: Die berufsbildende Schule (BbSch) *[The "Vocational School"]* 68 (2016) 1.

World Bank (2008): Skill Development in India – The vocational education and training system. URL: https://openknowledge.worldbank.org/bitstream/handle/10986/17937/423150India0VET0no02201PUBLIC1.pdf?sequence=1&isAllowed=y [6 October 2017]

World Bank (2017a): Population total. URL: http://data.worldbank.org/indicator/SP.POP.TOTL?end=2015&locations=IN&start=2015&view=map&year_low_desc=false [6 October 2017]

World Bank (2017b): Population, female (% of total). URL: http://data.worldbank.org/indicator/SP.POP.TOTL.FE.ZS?end=2015&locations=IN&start=1960&view=chart&year_high_desc=false [6 October 2017]

World Bank (2017c): GPD (current US$). URL: http://data.worldbank.org/indicator/NY.GDP.MKTP.CD?locations=IN&year_high_desc=false [6 October 2017]

World Bank (2017d): GPD per capita (current US$). URL: http://data.worldbank.org/indicator/NY.GDP.PCAP.CD?locations=IN&year_high_desc=false. [6 October 2017]

World Bank (2017e): Unemployment total (% of total labor force) (modelled ILO estimate). URL: http://data.worldbank.org/indicator/SL.UEM.TOTL.ZS?locations=IN&year_high_desc=false [6 October 2017]

World Bank (year of publication not stated, a). Indien: Altersstruktur von 2004 bis 2015 *[India – age structure from 2004 to 2015]*. URL: https://de.statista.com/statistik/daten/studie/170740/umfrage/altersstruktur-in-indien/ [6 October 2017]

World Bank (year of publication not stated, b). Indien: Alphabetisierungsgrad von 1981 bis 2015 *[India – degree of literacy from 1981 to 2005]*. URL: https://de.statista.com/statistik/daten/studie/170863/umfrage/alphabetisierung-in-indien/ [6 October 2017]

World Bank (year of publication not stated, c). Indien: Anteile der Wirtschaftssektoren am Bruttoinlandsprodukt (BIP) von 2005 bis 2015 *[India – share of economic sectors in Gross Domestic Product (GDP) from 2005 to 2015]*. URL: https://de.statista.com/statistik/daten/studie/170838/umfrage/anteile-der-wirtschaftssektoren-am-bruttoinlandsprodukt-indiens/ [6 October 2017]

World Bank (year of publication not stated d). Indien: Verteilung der Erwerbstätigen auf die Wirtschaftssektoren in den Jahren 1994, 2000, 2005, 2010, 2012 und 2013 *[India – distribution of labour demand to economic sectors in the years 1994, 2000, 2005, 2010, 2012 and 2013]*. URL: https://de.statista.com/statistik/daten/studie/170802/umfrage/erwerbstaetige-nach-wirtschaftssektoren-in-indien/ [6 October 2017]

World Bank; ILO (2013): Possible Futures for the Indian Apprenticeship System – Options Paper for India. URL: http://www.ilo.org/wcmsp5/groups/public/---asia/---ro-bangkok/---sro-new_delhi/documents/publication/wcms_234727.pdf [6 October 2017]

Zenner, Lea; Pilz, Matthias (2015): „Make in India" – Wie indische Unternehmen ausbilden *["Make in India"—how Indian companies provide training]*. In: Berufsbildung – Zeitschrift für Praxis und Theorie in Betrieb und Schule *[Vocational Education and Training – Journal for Practice and Theory in Companies and Schools]*, Vol. 69, Issue 154, pp. 7–9.

7 Further information

7.1 Legal foundations, training regulations, curricular materials

Relevant documents are mentioned in Chapter 3 and in Chapter 4.3 and can usually be accessed on the homepage of the respective Indian government institution (see also CBSE 2015 or http://cbse.nic.in/).

7.2 Addresses

Ministry of Skill Development and Entrepreneurship (MSDE)
2nd Floor, Annexe Building Shivaji Stadium
Shaheed Bhagat Singh Marg, Connaught Place
New Delhi – 110001
India
www.skilldevelopment.gov.in

Ministry of Human Resource Development (MHRD)
Department Of Higher Education
Shri S.P. Goyal
Joint Secretary (NITs & DL)
Shastri Bhawan
New Delhi – 110001
India
www.mhrd.gov.in

Department Of School Education & Literacy
Shri Manish Garg
Joint Secretary (SE-I)
Shastri Bhawan
New Delhi – 110001
India
www.mhrd.gov.in

Ministry of Labour and Employment (MoLE)
Govt. of India
Shram Shakti Bhawan
Rafi Marg
New Delhi-110001
India
www.labour.nic.in

National Institute of Open Schooling (NIOS)
A-24/25
Institutional Area
Sector - 62
NOIDA
Distt. Gautam Budh Nagar, Uttar Pradesh - 201 309
India
www.nos.org

Directorate General of Training (DGT)
Ministry of Skill Development and Entrepreneurship
Shram Shakti Bhawan
Rafi Marg, New Delhi-110001
India
www.dget.nic.in

7.3 Internet addresses

Ministry of Skill Development and Entrepreneurship: http://msde.gov.in
Ministry of Human Resource Development: www.mhrd.gov.in
Directorate General of Training: www.dget.nic.in/
All India Council for Technical Education: www.aicte-india.org
University Grants Commission: http://www.ugc.ac.in/
The National Institute of Open Schooling: www.nios.ac.in

Index of keywords

In the interests of better accessibility, the original Indian (English-language) designations have been used for the keyword index.

Organigram of the Educational System

- Labour market transition
- Direct
- Partly direct
- Rarely direct
- Share of practical training
- Entrance qualification
- Vocational education and training

- **N** Compulsory school leaving certificate
- **H** Tertiary entrance qualification
- **[H]** Limited tertiary entrance qualification
- **B/M** Higher education degree (bachelor/master)
- **B** Certificate engineering college (bachelor)
- **D** Certificate Polytechnic (Diploma)
- **T** Technician
- **F** Skilled worker
- **H** Skilled craftsmen
- **A** Unskilled

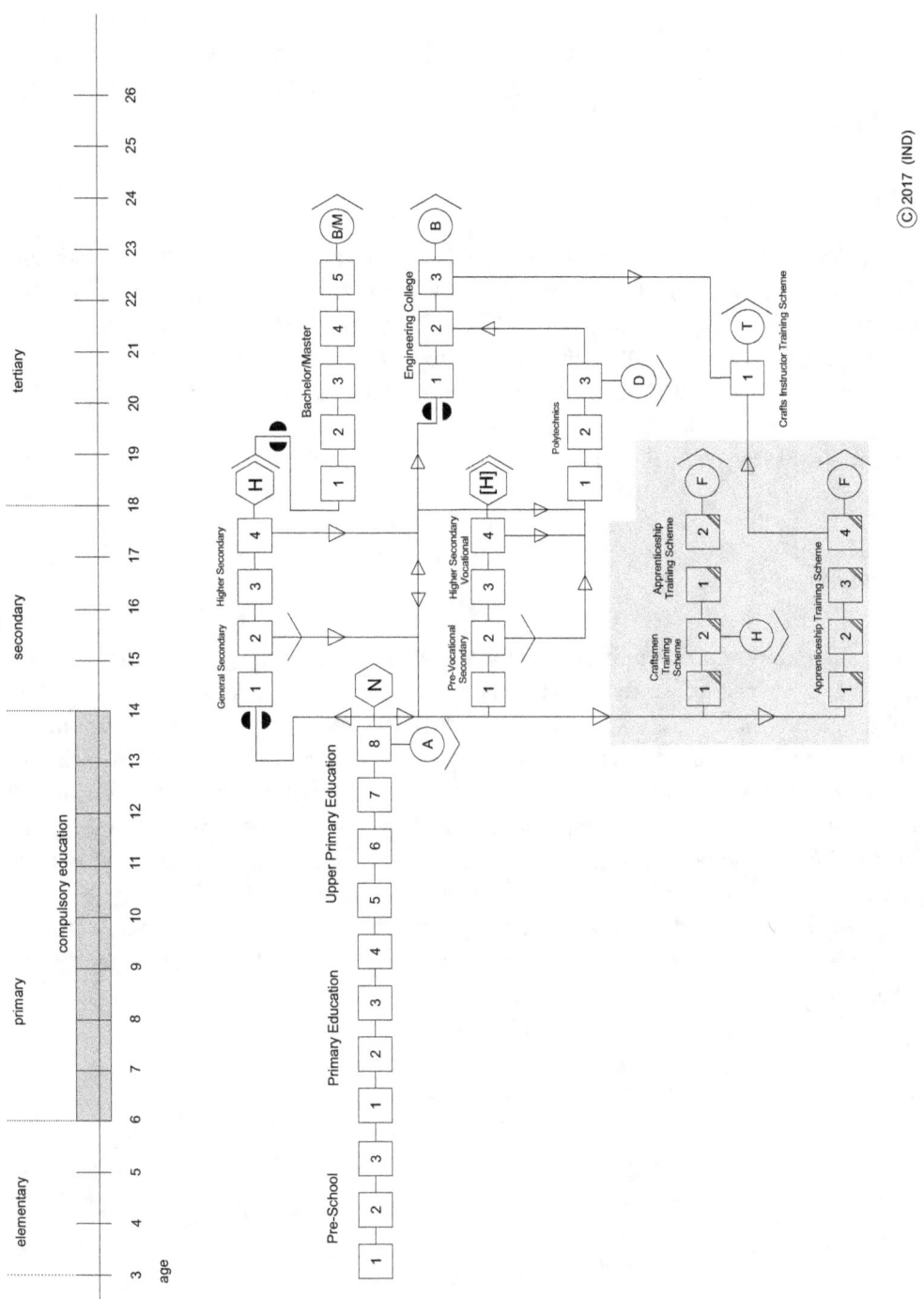

Authors

Antje Wessels, Faculty of Business and Social Education at the University of Cologne
Professor Matthias Pilz, Faculty of Business and Social Education at the University of Cologne

Editors

Verena Schneider, Dr Philipp Grollmann (content), Federal Institute for Vocational Education and Training (BIBB), Bonn, Dr Uwe Lauterbach (content), formerly of the German Institute for International Pedagogical Research (DIPF), Frankfurt am Main, Markus Linten (research), Dr Britta Nelskamp (proofreading), Federal Institute for Vocational Education and Training, Bonn, Boris Pipiorke-Arndt (graphics)

Completion/status: April 2017

Abstract

With a population of 1.3 billion, India is the world's second largest country and, from a Western perspective, an exotic country of many contrasts and with a very different culture. Since the 1990s, wide-ranging reforms have taken effect and the economic development of the country has gathered pace at many levels. Vocational education and training in India has therefore also come under the spotlight and must take account of the resulting challenges. Companies from Western countries as well as stakeholders involved in vocational education and training are active in India. In addition to the particular cultural aspects of the country, the vocational education and training landscape is largely characterised by Anglo-American concepts, a distinct tendency towards university education, a low level of participation by business and a complex management structure.

GPSR Authorized Representative: Easy Access System Europe, Mustamäe tee
50, 10621 Tallinn, Estonia, gpsr.requests@easproject.com

www.ingramcontent.com/pod-product-compliance
Lightning Source LLC
Chambersburg PA
CBHW081721120626
46550CB00010B/3191